BASKETBALL
Fun & Games

50 Skill-Building Activities for Children

Keven A. Prusak

Human Kinetics

Library of Congress Cataloging-in-Publication Data

Prusak, Keven A., 1960-
  Basketball fun & games : 50 skill-building activities for children / Keven A. Prusak.
    p. cm.
  ISBN 0-7360-4516-3 (soft cover)
  1. Basketball for children--Training. 2. Basketball for children--Coaching. I. Title:
Basketball fun and games. II. Title.
  GV886.25.P88 2005
  796.332'62--dc22

                              2004020850

ISBN: 0-7360-4516-3

Acquisitions Editor: Bonnie Pettifor; **Developmental Editor:** Jacqueline Eaton Blakley; **Assistant
Editors:** Bethany J. Bentley and Kathleen D. Bernard; **Copyeditor:** Amie Bell; **Proofreader:** Sue
Fetters; **Permission Manager:** Dalene Reeder; **Graphic Designer:** Fred Starbird; **Graphic Art-
ist:** Kathleen Boudreau-Fuoss; **Photo Manager:** Kelly J. Huff; **Cover Designer:** Keith Blomberg;
Photographer (cover): Tom Roberts; **Photos (interior):** Kelly J. Huff; **Art Manager:** Kelly Hen-
dren; **Illustrators:** Accurate Art and Kathleen Boudreau-Fuoss; **Printer:** United Graphics

Printed in the United States of America   10 9 8 7 6 5 4 3 2 1

Human Kinetics
Web site: www.HumanKinetics.com

United States: Human Kinetics
P.O. Box 5076, Champaign, IL 61825-5076
800-747-4457
e-mail: humank@hkusa.com

Canada: Human Kinetics
475 Devonshire Road Unit 100
Windsor, ON N8Y 2L5
800-465-7301 (in Canada only)
e-mail: orders@hkcanada.com

Europe: Human Kinetics
107 Bradford Road, Stanningley
Leeds LS28 6AT, United Kingdom
+44 (0) 113 255 5665
e-mail: hk@hkeurope.com

Australia: Human Kinetics
57A Price Avenue, Lower Mitcham
South Australia 5062
08 8277 1555
e-mail: liaw@hkaustralia.com

New Zealand: Human Kinetics
Division of Sports Distributors NZ Ltd.
P.O. Box 300 226 Albany
North Shore City, Auckland
0064 9 448 1207
e-mail: blairc@hknewz.com

CONTENTS

ACTIVITY FINDER

The Activity Finder (page vi) will help you find the activities that suit your kids' age and abilities and teach the desired skills quickly and easily. All of the activities are arranged in the Activity Finder in the order that they appear in the chapters. If, for example, you need a warm-up activity, look through the first eight activities and choose the desired skills, grade level, and difficulty level that suits your situation. The page number of your chosen activity is in the last column.

Important note: Some activities develop multiple skills. Most of these activities are included in chapter 6, Multiskill Activities, but some are listed in the chapter that most represents its focus. For example, see the pass-and-duck relay activity in chapter 4. This activity is mainly built around passing skills, thus the activity is listed in the chapter that focuses on passing. However, the activity also uses a variety of dribbling skills.

Activity Finder Key

Skills Involved in the Activity

D	Defensive	**S**	Shooting
B	Ball handling, Dribbling	**F**	Footwork
P	Passing	**R**	Rebounding
T	Tactical, Teamwork, Strategies		

No.	Name	Skills	Grades	Page
1	Move and Freeze	F	K-6	8
2	Marking	F	5-6	11
3	Fugitive Tag	F, T	3-6	13
4	Fastest Dribble Tag	B, P, S	5-6	14
5	Rings of Fire	B, D, F	2-5	16
6	Dribble Tip Over	B, T	4-6	18
7	Ball-Handling Series	B	3-6	19
8	Disappearing Islands	B, F	K-6	22
9	Four-Call Dribbling	B, T	5-6	26
10	Dribble Dance	B, T	4-5	30
11	Sharks and Minnows	B, D, T	4-6	32
12	Two-Ball Dribbling	B, F	5-6	34
13	Blinking Game	B, T	3-5	36
14	Dribbling and Juggling	B	4-6	37
15	Dribbling Hoops	All	K-2	38
16	Triangle Footwork	F, B	3-6	42
17	Clone Dribbling	B, F	5-6	44
18	Five Passes	P, T, F	K-6	48
19	Partner Passing	P	3-6	50
20	Team Passing Challenge	P	5-6	53
21	Pass-and-Duck Relay	P	5-6	54
22	Cannon Shot	S, P	5-6	56
23	Partner Wall Passing	P	5-6	58
24	Twenty-One	S, T, P	4-6	62

PREFACE

"Oh, I hate basketball!"

So said a fifth-grade student in a physical education class I was guest teaching when I told them we would be playing basketball that day. But after playing several games that I've included in this book, she and several others asked if I could come back because they had never had so much fun playing basketball.

Isn't this result exactly what we want as physical education practitioners—for kids to actually enjoy learning vital fitness, skills, and games? So often, the missing ingredient is fun. If we can make learning fun, we can increase the effectiveness of our teaching.

When I lead teacher training workshops across the country, I inevitably hear from teachers, "That was fun! Where can I get more activities like this one?" Teachers and youth coaches are hungry for new age- and developmentally appropriate activities. They don't always have the time to create and test new activities. Some teachers feel that they are "just not that creative." Some rely on activities from their own past experience that are poorly suited to the age of their students. Many are tired of old drills and are looking for a fun way to improve their students' skills and fitness.

This book is a collection of favorite activities that I have shared over the years with physical educators and youth sport coaches across the United States. Twenty years of teaching physical education, coaching basketball, and conducting research in physical education has taught me a few things:

• **Kids just want to have fun.** Physical education is undergoing a remarkable transition from a sports-based curriculum to one of physical activity. Youth sports are ever more focused on providing a positive competitive experience and encouraging success for all participants, which in turn increases kids' motivation. Parents, administrators, and recreational leaders are recognizing what children have always wanted from participating in physical education: to have fun. The activities in this book have been designed to provide quality learning experiences in a fun and engaging way. Teachers and coaches have the power to create an environment that kids thrive in, gaining greater skill and fitness and loving every minute of it. This book can help you as you seek to fulfill that goal.

• **Competition doesn't always bring out the best in kids.** Basketball is a competitive activity, so it can be difficult to provide a positive experience for all students, particularly for those with less ability. Children and youth want to compare favorably to their peers, but to do so takes time and practice. Drills that place a child in front of his or her peers before the child's skills are proficient lead to a negative experience. That's why this book offers drills and activities that help students become skilled by maximizing the number of practice attempts while minimizing peer comparison. Later, as skills are more and more proficient, increasing and appropriate levels of competition are incorporated into the activities. This evolution promotes learning to be a capable competitor without feeling anxiety due to inappropriate emphasis on winning and losing as the sole indicator of success.

• **Conditioning and skill building can be accomplished simultaneously.** Sport conditioning is a critical aspect of successful competition, and fitness is a vital goal for physical educators. Typically, physical educators treat conditioning and skill building as separate activities, but it doesn't have to be this way. It's possible to develop skill and fitness simultaneously, and the activities in this book are designed to do exactly that. For example, while they do these activities, students can be increasing their cardiovascular endurance and becoming more accurate shooters. The bonus of skill–fitness activities is the increased motivation students have toward engaging in vigorous physical activity when a ball is placed in their hands.

It is my hope that this book will provide you with many useful activities for teaching and coaching children in basketball. Although each of these activities has been developed and used with kids in kindergarten through sixth grades, I suggest that you further refine the activity to suit your own circumstances. I further hope that the principles underlying the development of these activities, as explained in chapter 1, will help you refine your present drills, making them even better, more productive, and enjoyable for kids. Then I hope that you will share these activities with colleagues so that others will benefit from them as well.

ACKNOWLEDGMENTS

I would like to acknowledge the contribution of many people who have made this book a reality. Thanks to Bonnie Pettifor, Jackie Blakley, and Human Kinetics for their invitation to author a book in this series. Thanks to Bob Pangrazi for his guidance and confidence in recommending me for the project. I am grateful to Don Meyers, who is a coach's coach, and is ever willing to share his ideas, which are always topnotch.

KEY TO DIAGRAMS

Offensive player	○
Defensive player	✕
Different teams	A, B, C, D, and so on
Coach	C
Run or sprint	——————▶
Pass	- - - - - -▶
Shoot	·············▶
Dribble	∿∿∿▶
Screen	———————⊣
Slide	⇒
Backpedal	✕✕✕✕✕✕▶
Poly spots	🔘 ⊘ ⚫
Cones	△
Hoops	○

CHAPTER 1

INTRODUCTION

This book contains 50 age- and developmentally appropriate activities that can be incorporated into any educational or coaching setting. The activities are designed to help children accomplish three major goals: (1) be highly active, (2) be highly successful, and (3) have lots of fun all while learning the game of basketball. All three goals must be met in every activity for children to realize the maximum benefit. Let me elaborate.

1. **Children need to be highly active!** Kids should be moving. You want children in your classes to be breathing hard, with pink little cheeks and hearts that are pounding. High activity allows for the health and sports conditioning benefits to be realized. Equally important, you want kids to receive the

maximum number of skill-building repetitions. Kids should have the ball in their hands as much as possible. Avoid having the kids standing in lines or taking turns as much as you can. You will find in this book a collection of dynamic and engaging activities that allow all kids to be active at the same time. To help each child to gain the maximum benefits of fitness and skill acquisition, many of the activities in this book combine skill learning and fitness into a skill–fitness activity. Kids will enjoy a fitness activity much more if they have a ball in their hand while doing it. And, while they are getting fit, they are also becoming more skilled.

2. **Children want to feel highly successful!** Because these activities focus on the learning process they allow kids to succeed all or most of the time. The activities build within individual kids solid work habits that focus on working at something until you can do it rather than having to measure up to those around you. The pressure of performing a skill in front of others is, for the most part, reserved until skills are proficient.

3. **Children want to have a lot of fun!** The whole idea of this book centers on the idea that learning to play the game of basketball can be a really enjoyable experience. Drills do not have to be drudgery. In fact, just about any drill can be modified to meet the three goals of high activity, high success, and high enjoyment. If we provide a positive experience in which students have high incidences of practice and success they will have more fun learning the game. Indeed, the overwhelming reason that kids choose to participate fully in the first place is so they can have fun.

The activities in *Basketball Fun & Games* focus on building individual skills that lead to team success. The activities are generally grouped according to fundamental basketball and team-sports skills:

- Warming up
- Ball handling
- Passing
- Shooting
- Multiskill activities
- Tactics and teamwork

Each activity outlines the information you need to know to conduct it, including the following elements:

• **Time.** A suggested amount of time is indicated for each activity. Note that these activities are generally short and may be repeated or adjusted if time and circumstances allow.

• **National standards.** Each activity helps kids achieve one or more of the National Association for Sport & Physical Education (NASPE)'s national standards for physical education. The standards are shown here for your reference:

1. Demonstrates competency in motor skills and movement patterns needed to perform a variety of physical activities
2. Demonstrates understanding of movement concepts, principles, strategies, and tactics as they apply to the learning and performance of physical activities
3. Participates regularly in physical activity
4. Achieves and maintains a health-enhancing level of physical activity
5. Exhibits responsible personal and social behavior that respects self and others in physical activity settings
6. Values physical activity for health, enjoyment, challenge, self-expression, and/or social interaction

Reprinted from *Moving into the Future: National Standards for Physical Education*, 2nd edition, with permission from the National Association for Sport and Physical Education (NASPE), 1900 Association Drive, Reston, VA 20191, USA.

• **Level.** Each activity is designed to be age- and developmentally appropriate for the level indicated. Although the word *level* in this book indicates grades kindergarten through six (K-6), age groups in K-6 are commonly divided into three developmental levels: K-2, 3-4, and 5-6. You may use the indicated level as a general guideline for both age and developmental levels. However, feel free to adjust the activities to suit your specific needs.

• **Objectives.** Each activity is designed with basketball-specific objectives and outcomes in mind. Consult the stated objectives and keep them in mind when selecting and implementing an activity.

• **Equipment.** Amount and type of equipment are listed next. Equipment should be well maintained and serviceable and selected to suit the age and developmental level of the students. It is always a good practice to survey the equipment and activity space before beginning instruction to ensure safety and the proper functioning of equipment.

It is more important that each student have a piece of equipment that is serviceable than it is to have the best, most up-to-date equipment available. Generally, buying greater quantities of less expensive basketballs is better than purchasing a smaller number of high-quality leather basketballs, particularly for younger students. Balls come in a variety of sizes to suit particular age and developmental needs. Other equipment mentioned, such as poly spots, hula hoops, and cones, are all commonly found at a variety of vendor sources. Choose those suited to your specific needs.

Modifying equipment size, spacing, and height is encouraged to result in greater student success. Remember that small-group or individual activities ought to be the norm, thus requiring more equipment; ideally, every student should have a ball or piece of equipment. These activities often involve creating station signs as a means to increase the type and frequency of information and feedback to students when the coach may be occupied elsewhere, resulting in more self-directed learning. Occasionally, the activity suggests the use of timed music, which increases the student enjoyment and helps to manage the activity. I recommend that you create, in advance, a variety of taped music or CDs. Generally, these drills do not require a great deal of equipment, but at times they do require a variety of equipment.

• **Description.** Step-by-step instructions are provided to help you manage and conduct each activity in a time-efficient and clear manner. Children, with their short attention spans, learn best in short, intermittent episodes. Therefore, give few but very clear instructions and begin the activity immediately, adding and clarifying as needed throughout. Keeping the directions concise avoids long, drawn-out instructions that students may not be able to remember and follow.

• **Variations.** Although each of the activities contains a suggested level, it is possible to modify almost all of them to suit any age level. Suggested modifications are often included in the activity, but I encourage you to make further changes to suit your teaching needs.

• **Teaching tips.** The success of any activity requires first and foremost that teachers and coaches be *effective managers of kids and the setting*. Learning objectives fall away when time is wasted due to poor management skills. The step-by-step descriptions also include specific language intended to help you manage more effectively. Keep in mind the following general management guidelines (specific teaching tips may also be listed with each activity):

- Set up your teaching station beforehand to be safe and facilitate the flow of the lesson.
- Meet the kids at the door with a short greeting and then hit the ground running.
- Use movement to manage kids, knowing that problems arise when children are standing around with nothing to do.
- Choose consistent starting and stopping signals and use them every time.
- Make quick transitions (either to move equipment or to establish groups and formations) in under 30 seconds.
- When giving instructions, always tell the students the *when* before the *what*. For example, you might say, "Class, when I say go, jog over to the wall, get a ball, return to your own space on the floor, and begin dribbling. Go!" This sequencing ensures that students hear all of the instructions.
- Give only enough instructions to get the activity going and then add on to the activity throughout the drill.

Now you're ready to proceed with the activities. Best of luck, and above all . . . have fun!

CHAPTER 2

WARMING UP

Class time is limited, so don't waste a minute of it by having kids run laps just to warm up. Sure, they will warm up by running laps—but they could have gotten so much more. Warm-up time can also be a time for developing skills and good work habits. The activities presented here provide a proper warm-up in a way that captures student interest while providing extra practice attempts. These activities involve body movement and ball-handling skills straight from the game of basketball. Be sure to follow a brief warm-up with stretching the warm muscles, tendons, and ligaments. Intersperse these warm-up activities with regular upper- and lower-body stretches.

1 Move and Freeze

Time	National Standards	Grades
2-3 minutes	1, 5	K-2 and 3-6, with variations to movements

OBJECTIVES

1. Warm up large muscle groups, tendons, and ligaments and prepare the body for flexibility exercises or more vigorous activities to follow
2. Practice simple gross-motor movements that use large muscle groups, are easy to do, and promote success
3. Practice basketball-specific locomotor movements as well as changes of direction and speed to build agility and balance
4. Explore spacing and working in a responsible manner in one's own space
5. Listen and respond to instructions

EQUIPMENT

None

DESCRIPTION

In this activity students will practice a variety of movements and skills according to your signals. Move and Freeze is a great way to hit the ground running and set the tone for the rest of your lesson by using activity to manage kids.

1. Meet the students at the door and say, "When you hear the whistle today, please freeze with your hands on your knees, eyes on me, tummies facing me, and voices off." Model the position you want them to take by performing a two-feet jump stop, placing your hands on your knees, then zipping your lips with one hand. Have students practice this move in place two times. (You may also use the command "Freeze!" as the signal.) Then instruct, "When I say, 'Go,' please come into the gym jogging in your own space. Go!"

2. As the students begin to jog into the gym, reinforce jogging safely throughout the entire space of the gym, changing directions often. Once all have entered, give the freeze signal and model the freeze position. Scan from one side of the gym to the other, reinforcing two or three students who complied correctly and quickly.

3. Now that the students are listening, say, "We are going to practice a variety of basketball movements and skills in our warm-up today. Remember to freeze on the signal, and then I will give you another movement to do. When I say, 'Go,' begin skipping using the whole gym. Remember to be safe and change directions often. Go!" Move throughout the gym picking out individuals and giving reinforcement and feedback.

4. Repeat this procedure: (a) freeze, (b) scan, (c) reinforce, and (d) model a different skill or movement you want the students to practice, and (e) say, "Go!" Skills you might have K-2 students practice include the following:

> Walking
>
> Skipping
>
> Galloping
>
> Sliding to the side
>
> Sprinting
>
> Hopping (one foot)
>
> Jumping (two feet)
>
> Leaping
>
> Stopping and pivoting

Older students (grades 3-6) can practice more advanced skills and movement in combination such as those listed next:

> Jog in place
>
> Jump stop followed by a change of directions or by a pivot
>
> Jump shot and then return to a jog
>
> Slide to one side; jump stop; and perform a basketball skill such as shooting, passing, or dribbling

Be creative in combining skills into ever more complex patterns that more closely resemble the game. After the students have practiced the skill and need a change (about 10 to 30 seconds), freeze and introduce a new movement.

TEACHING TIPS

- A good rule of thumb when giving instructions is to tell students *when* before *what*. For example, say, "When I say, 'Go,' please begin skipping throughout the space." This sequencing ensures that students hear all of the instructions before beginning the activity.

- Keep instructions short. Kids have short attention spans, and it is often best to give short instructions and get them going with the activity. Then observe their actions to check for understanding and make any necessary adjustments.

- Model more and talk less when giving instructions.

- Reinforce the importance of using the entire gym, allowing lots of room to move, changing directions, controlling one's body, and being safe. Running laps is discouraged as it stifles student creativity and their need to assess and react to the ever-changing environment.

- Be sure that students understand which signal(s) will be used and use them consistently throughout the activity.

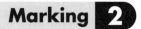
Time	National Standards	Grades
2-4 minutes (allowing equal time for each partner to do both parts)	1, 5, 6	5-6

OBJECTIVES

1. Warm up large muscle groups, tendons, and ligaments and prepare the body for flexibility exercises or more vigorous activities to follow
2. Use a variety of locomotor movements to practice agility and balance specific to the game of basketball
3. Cooperate with another student by filling and changing roles during the activity
4. Explore the simple defensive concept of staying close to one's defensive assignment
5. Learn about the appropriate levels of competition, fairness of play, and cooperation

EQUIPMENT

None

DESCRIPTION

1. Pair up students according to size and abilities, designating a partner 1 and partner 2 in each pair. Have the pairs scatter throughout the space.
2. Explain, "When I say, 'Go,' partner 1 will execute the movement or skill I name. Partner 2 will do the same movement, trying to stay within reaching distance of partner 1. When you hear the whistle, everybody freeze with a two-feet jump stop. Then partner 2 will try to reach out and touch partner 1. Any partner 2 who can touch his or her partner receives a point; if partner 2 cannot touch partner 1, partner 1 receives a point." Partner 1 practices a variety of dynamic movements such as dodging, zigzagging (V-cuts), and evading. Partner 2 practices

like skills along with maintaining a proper defensive closeness (arm's length) to his or her partner.

3. Have partners stand close to one another. Call out a skill or movement (walk, jog, run, skip, slide, jump, hop, dodging, zig-zagging, evading, and so on), demonstrate the movement, and say, "Go!" Partner 1 performs the movement and tries to get away from her or his partner; partner 2 does the same movement and tries to stay within reaching distance of partner 1. Give the stop signal and see who scored the point and keep track of the score.

4. Have the partners switch roles and repeat an equal number of times for each partner.

TEACHING TIPS

- Partners start close to one another.
- Remind the students that on the whistle, players must come to an immediate two-feet jump stop and cannot move their feet when attempting to tag their partner.
- Remind students to move safely throughout the space, avoiding other couples.
- Winners must give a high five to partners when the game ends.

Time	National Standards	Grades
3-5 minutes (allowing equal time for each partner to do both parts)	1, 5, 7	3-6

OBJECTIVES

1. Warm up large muscle groups, tendons, and ligaments and prepare the body for flexibility exercises or more vigorous activities to follow
2. Work cooperatively with other students
3. Use a variety of basketball-specific locomotor movements to practice agility and balance
4. Explore simple defensive concepts of viewing the entire court, assessing and responding to an ever-changing situation, and formulating and executing a plan of attack

EQUIPMENT

None

DESCRIPTION

1. Pair up students according to size and abilities, designating a partner 1 and partner 2 in each pair.
2. Have all partner 1s (the detectives) go to the center of the gym, face the center, and cover their eyes. Partner 2s (the fugitives) "escape" by moving throughout the space with a locomotor movement you choose and trying to avoid their partners.
3. On the command—"Detectives, find your fugitive!"—the detectives open their eyes and then must locate and tag their partner to capture them.
4. Have partners switch roles and repeat an equal number of times. Choose different locomotor movements.

TEACHING TIP

Remind students to move safely throughout the space, avoiding other couples.

Time	National Standards	Grades
2-3 minutes (this is enough time to repeat several times)	1, 5, 6	5-6

OBJECTIVES

1. Warm up large muscle groups, tendons, and ligaments and prepare the body for flexibility exercises or more vigorous activities to follow
2. Practice dribbling skills in a gamelike situation
3. Experience a sense of urgency and light competition

EQUIPMENT

One ball per student

DESCRIPTION

This game goes very fast because all players are "it."

1. Have all players move throughout the half-court, dribbling while trying to tag other players and avoid being tagged themselves. A player who is tagged is out and must move to the outside of the half-court boundaries and dribble around the perimeter with her or his weak hand. The last person still in the game wins.
2. If two players tag each other at the same time, both players are out. If a player loses control of the ball or steps out of bounds, he or she is out.
3. In order to prolong the game and keep all players active and interested, you can "recycle" tagged players:
   - The player may return to the game after completing one lap of dribbling around the perimeter.
   - The player may move to the other half-court and begin to play there. (If tagged there, the player may return to the original half-court and continue playing.)

- The player may return to the game after making three free throws.

You may allow students to take a "safe" position, such as kneeling down while dribbling, moving the ball around the waist, or any other skill you wish them to practice. A student in danger of being tagged may stay in the safe position for a maximum of 5 seconds.

5 Rings of Fire

Time	National Standards	Grades
4-6 minutes	1, 2, 5	2-5

OBJECTIVES

1. Dribble while moving successfully in traffic
2. Learn to protect the ball from defenders
3. Learn to try to steal the ball from offenders without committing a foul

EQUIPMENT

One ball for half the class, one poly spot (or hoops) for the other half of the class

DESCRIPTION

1. Spread poly spots throughout an open space. Divide class into two teams. Team 1 players stand on each spot with both feet.
2. Team 2 students move throughout the space, dribbling around the poly spots without bumping into the students on the spots or each other. The players on the poly spots cannot interfere with the dribblers as they move throughout the space.
3. When the players are comfortable and successful in dribbling among the spots, announce that the poly spots are "on fire," meaning that team 1 players may try to tap the ball away from the dribblers (team 2). Instruct team 1 to use their hands only, to keep both feet on the spot, and to tap the ball and not the dribbler (touching the dribbler is a foul). Instruct team 2 to use correct dribbling skills and protect the ball (change hands, direction, or speed, and so on) as they move throughout the space.
4. If fouled, the dribbler continues without interruption. If a dribbler loses the ball, he may regain control of the ball and continue, or, as a variation, move to the perimeter and perform a prescribed skill and then return.
5. Play for 20 to 30 seconds, then have players reverse roles. Dribblers should try to maintain possession for the entire time.

VARIATION

As players' skills improve, move the spots closer together to lessen the dribbling space.

Author: Joshua Guthrie; adapted by permission of PE Central (www.pecentral.org), the premier Web site for physical educators.

6 Dribble Tip Over

Time	National Standards	Grades
3-5 minutes	1, 2, 5	4-6

OBJECTIVES

1. Practice dribbling while looking up
2. Maintain awareness of surroundings
3. Compete as a team while working toward a common goal

EQUIPMENT

One ball per person; 10-15 cones or bowling pins

DESCRIPTION

1. Place an equal number of cones upright within each half of a basketball court. Divide players into two teams.

2. When you give the signal, players on team 1 dribble while using the nondribbling hand to knock over as many cones as possible. If a player loses control of the ball, he or she must return the cone to its upright position before recovering the ball.

3. Team 2 players dribble while returning the cones to an upright position. If a player loses control of the ball, he or she must tip the cone over again before recovering the ball.

4. After 30 seconds, signal players to stop. One point is awarded to team 2 for each cone still standing. Teams reverse roles and play again. Remember to give an equal number of turns to each team.

Author: John Pinder; adapted by permission of PE Central (www.pecentral.org), the premier Web site for physical educators.

Time	National Standards	Grades
5-7 minutes	1, 2, 3	3-6

OBJECTIVES

1. Warm up large muscle groups, tendons, and ligaments and prepare the body for flexibility exercises or more vigorous activities to follow
2. Practice basketball-specific movements
3. Practice ball-handling skills in a fast-paced manner
4. Experience success and challenge current skill levels

EQUIPMENT

One age- and size-appropriate ball per student

DESCRIPTION

1. Say to students, "Get a ball, find a space on the floor, and begin moving the ball counterclockwise around your waist like this." Demonstrate how the students should move the ball. Once students have completed 5 to 10 seconds or revolutions say, "Change directions," and model moving the ball clockwise. Give the signal to stop (either blow your whistle or say, "Freeze!"). Model and tell students, "When we freeze with a ball we place our ball on the floor and back away." Students above fourth grade may hold the ball under one arm instead of placing it on the floor.
2. Now say, "Please keep eyes on me wherever I go throughout the gym. When I say, 'Go,' pick up your ball and move it counterclockwise around your knees like this. Go!" After 5 to 10 seconds or revolutions, say, "Change directions," and model moving the ball clockwise.
3. Have the students do the following activities sequentially, following your modeling and cues:
   a. Move the ball around the head in both directions (see photo *a* on page 21).
   b. Move the ball around the knees, waist, and head, working upward and then downward (see photo *b* on page 21).

c. Move the ball around the left knee (both directions). Switch knees.

d. Move the ball around both knees in a figure-8 pattern in both directions (see photo *c* on page 21).

e. Stagger feet front to back. Pass the ball through the legs, and then change feet and pass the ball back through the legs from the other direction (keep head up).

f. Pass the ball through the legs while walking forward (keep head up). Repeat while running forward.

g. Dribble through the legs while changing feet. (This is the point where you may need to begin slowing the drills.)

h. Dribble through the legs while walking (see photo *d* on page 21).

i. Stand with wide feet. Dribble a figure-8 around both feet (both directions).

j. Stand with wide feet. Toss and catch the ball with two hands through the legs, front to back. (You may need to speed up the drills here.)

k. Stand with wide feet. Toss and catch between the legs with one hand in front and one in back, switching hands each time.

l. Stand with wide feet. Practice spider dribbling: Dribble between the feet with two taps in front followed by two taps in back.

TEACHING TIPS

- Instruct the students to turn to see you as you move throughout the gym.

- Begin with the simplest activity and progress to the more difficult. Move quickly (5 to 15 seconds) through the simpler activities to avoid boredom. Slow down (15 to 25 seconds) when the activities are becoming more challenging. Then move quickly again through the most challenging activities to avoid excessive frustration and failure.

- Emphasize good balance, keeping the eyes up and not on the ball, moving the ball in both directions, and using both hands equally.

8 Disappearing Islands

Time	National Standards	Grades
5-6 minutes	1, 2, 5, 6	K-6

OBJECTIVES

1. Warm up in a fun, engaging, and skill-based activity
2. Learn to see the entire floor and anticipate and respond to the movements of other players
3. Focus on a variety of dribbling skills

EQUIPMENT

Balls and hula hoops (islands) for each person, CDs or taped music with random intervals, CD or tape player (if you can't gain access to music, you can perform this activity by using verbal and whistle cues instead of stopping and starting music)

DESCRIPTION

1. This activity is similar to musical chairs. Have each player place a hoop on the floor (hoops should be scattered throughout the space) and begin dribbling throughout the spaces between the hoops. Start the music.
2. Remove one or more hoops (like musical chairs) while the players dribble. Call out the type of dribbling skill you want players to practice (for example, control dribble, speed dribble, dribbling in and out of hoops, dribbling with the nondominant hand). Change the type of dribble at your discretion.
3. On your signal or when the music stops, players must find a hoop, place one foot in it, and perform a dribbling challenge (for example, dribble with the nondominant hand around the hoop with one foot in and one foot out of the hoop). The players who are without hoops pick the next dribbling challenge to be done when the music stops again, and then they rejoin the activity. (In this way, no one is eliminated and those who are left without a hoop have a role to play and are not perceived as losers.)

4. When you start the music or give the signal, dribbling throughout the hoops begins again.

VARIATIONS

- You may allow older, more skilled students (fifth and sixth grade) to try to knock an opponent's ball away, adding to the difficulty faced by the dribblers.
- Two-ball dribbling is a great way to challenge the more advanced players. Allow the players to use random skills (change hands, crossover, reverse pivot, zigzag) as they move in the spaces between hoops. Call out the skills at random, or allow students to choose them as they wish. This variation in skills promotes making decisions on the go, as students must adjust to the ever-changing traffic around them.

TEACHING TIP

Remind players to keep their heads up and not watch the ball and to constantly read the position of other players on the floor and make quick, strategic decisions on the go.

CHAPTER 3

BALL HANDLING

Becoming familiar with the feel and handling of a basketball is perhaps the most fundamental of all basketball skills. This is accomplished best by getting as many touches with the ball in a variety of situations and activities. Being able to handle the ball while "looking up" is an especially important skill, as is handling the ball well with one's non-dominant hand. Handling the ball is not, however, restricted to one's hands; it involves the whole body. A variety of ball-handling skills are needed because basketball is a very dynamic, ever-changing sport. Skills change according to certain elements, such as the position of the ball in relation to one's body, to teammates and opponents, and to your position on the floor. Manipulating the ball while stationary, then adding movement, and progressing to interacting with others is an important development to help learn these changing skills. These activities will make handling the ball fun and will promote success.

Four-Call Dribbling

Time	National Standards	Grades
5-7 minutes	1, 2, 3, 4	5-6

OBJECTIVES

1. Develop heart and lung fitness and skills
2. Learn and practice four fundamental dribbling skills: control, power, speed, and backup
3. Develop ability to alternate dribbling techniques quickly

EQUIPMENT

One ball per student

DESCRIPTION

1. Say to your students, "Please get a ball, place your right foot on the sideline with your left foot in the court, and begin dribbling. When I blow the whistle or say, 'Freeze!' place the ball on the floor and back away." Older students may hold the ball under one arm. When all students are in place along the sideline and have dribbled for about 10 seconds, blow your whistle or say, "Freeze!" Explain to the students that you are going to teach them four fundamental dribbles and have them practice the dribbles with you.

2. Explain and demonstrate the control dribble (see photo *a* on page 28). Assume an athletic stance (knees slightly bent, feet shoulder-width apart) and turn sideways. Dribble rapidly at knee height and to the side of your back knee, keeping your head up and eyes forward. Instruct students to keep a "ball-me-you" relationship to the defender, that is, the dribbler should always try to keep himself between the ball and the defender. Say, "When I say, 'Control,' please start a control dribble with your right hand. When I say, 'Switch,' face the opposite direction and try the control dribble with your left hand." On your cues, the students practice the control dribble for about 15 seconds with each hand.

3. Explain and demonstrate the power dribble (see photo *b* on page 28). This is like a control dribble, but the dribbler advances across the court with a hippity-hop or a sideways-

sliding action. Reinforce the ball-me-you relationship. Say, "Follow my signals as we move across the court. I will call out control or power dribble and you follow." Lead the students across the court to the opposite sideline alternating control and power dribbles, verbally signaling them to switch at random intervals of 2 to 5 seconds. Use the right hand to go across to the other sideline, and then return using the left hand. Continue alternating control and power dribble until everyone reaches the original sideline.

4. Explain and demonstrate the speed dribble, which is used in fast-break game situations when the defender is behind you. Sprint across the court dribbling the ball high and out in front of you, maintaining the ball-me-you relationship to the defenders who are behind you (see photo *c* on page 29). Explain and demonstrate switching from speed dribble to control dribble: Flip both feet out in front of you and bring the ball back to a control dribble. This switch is accomplished by performing a two-feet jump-stop while moving the dribble behind the back knee as in control dribble. Switching from speed to control dribble is done when a defender cuts off the fast break and the ball handler must reestablish the ball-me-you relationship with the defender. Flipping the feet out in front is preferable to taking many steps to make the transition from speed to control dribble because it makes for a faster transition.

5. Say, "Listen for my calls as we move across the court again practicing the control dribble, power dribble (see photo *d* on page 29), and now speed dribble." Verbally cue the students to do a control dribble, then advance using the power dribble, then do a control dribble again, then sprint with a speed dribble. Continue various combinations of the three dribbles for 30 to 60 seconds across the court with the right hand and returning with the left hand.

6. Explain and demonstrate the backup dribble. Do this exactly like the power dribble, but move backward, away from the defender, maintaining the ball-me-you relationship.

7. Now that the students know all four of the dribbles, put them together in a series of calls that suit the abilities of your particular class. You can call for a speed dribble at any time, but always follow it with a control dribble call. Also, move across the floor using the right hand and return using the left hand.

VARIATIONS

- As the students get older or more proficient, give them less time between calls and present more challenging skills.
- Add a "switch" call in the middle of the floor and instruct students to change hands with a change-of-direction skill such as going through the legs.
- Instruct very skilled students to perform all skills with two balls.

TEACHING TIPS

- Encourage students to focus on doing the skill only as fast as they can do it correctly.
- Allow more time for younger students to perform the skill before making the next call.
- Once introduced, this makes an excellent warm-up or skill drill as well as a skill–fitness routine.

Adapted with permission of Don Meyer, Northern State University.

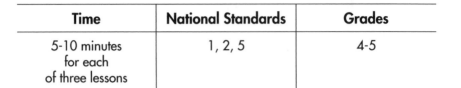

10 Dribble Dance

Time	National Standards	Grades
5-10 minutes for each of three lessons	1, 2, 5	4-5

OBJECTIVES

1. Develop dribbling skills
2. Work cooperatively with a partner
3. Develop creative and critical thinking skills
4. Execute skills in a sequence

EQUIPMENT

One ball, paper, pencil, and performance checklist for each student (students will create individual checklists for evaluating their own routines).

DESCRIPTION

A popular and entertaining form of basketball involves creating a series of dribbing moves together—like a dance. In some parts of the country, this has become so entertaining that large crowds come to watch not only the games but also these dribble dances during the game.

1. Pair up students with similar dribbling ability and instruct them to create a short dribbling routine with their partner. Encourage players to be creative and to work cooperatively while creating their routine. Using paper and pencil, partners will write down their routine in a series of movements that will serve as their checklist. They will present the checklist to the teacher or viewers and then perform the routine.

2. Outline some problem-solving parameters for the routine, including but not limited to the following:
   - Include three (or more) skills (your routine *must* include at least three skills).
   - Use both hands equally.

- Use eight counts (or beats) for each skill.
- Include stationary dribbling (for added challenge add mirroring; movement; or movement relationships, such as leading and following or alternating).
- Add fancy dribbling challenges for advanced players such as going through the legs, around the back, and so forth.
- Add passing challenges in which partners exchange balls in their routine.

3. Partners develop and write down their routine, then practice it to proficiency on days one and two. On day three, team up two groups of partners to perform their routines for each other. The viewers can assess the performance using the checklist. Instruct them to offer the performers at least one piece of positive feedback about the routine.

Author: Pete Anderson; used by permission of PE Central (www.pecentral.org), the premier Web site for physical educators.

Time	National Standards	Grades
4-5 minutes to repeat twice	1, 2, 5	4-6

OBJECTIVES

1. Practice defensive and offensive skills
2. Form strategies on the go
3. Practice dribbling through a gauntlet of defenders
4. Practice changes of direction and pace

EQUIPMENT

One ball per student

DESCRIPTION

1. Have players take a ball and line up along a sideline. Choose two or three "sharks" and station them around midcourt (see diagram). Have the sharks put away their balls.
2. Explain to all students that the sharks will defend against the "minnows"—the students along the sideline—as the minnows try to dribble across to the opposite sideline. The sharks must try to stop them by stealing their ball.
3. If a shark steals the ball, the minnow places his or her ball against the wall, becomes a shark, and now defends against the remaining minnows. If fouled, the minnow gets a free pass. Once a minnow reaches the opposite sideline, the minnow may return immediately to the original sideline or rest for up to twenty seconds.
4. The game continues until all minnows are caught. Minnows must use a variety of dribbling skills (control, power, speed, backup, changes of direction and pace) to avoid having their ball stolen.

VARIATIONS

• Have two minnows (or three minnows, or more) share and pass one ball as they try to make it across to the opposite sideline.

- Award a point for each safe trip across and see who can get the most points.

Sharks and Minnows makes a good warm-up activity, or you can have students use this as a short game at the end of class.

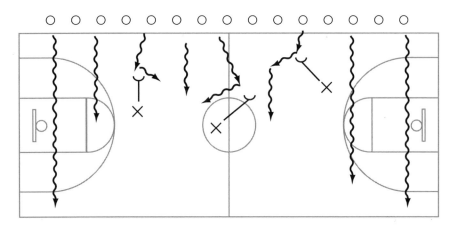

Used by permission of PE Central (www.pecentral.org), the premier Web site for physical educators.

12 Two-Ball Dribbling

Time	National Standards	Grades
4-6 minutes	1, 2	5-6

OBJECTIVES

1. Practice dribbling with both hands simultaneously and maximize practice efficiency
2. Learn to focus attention on more than one thing at a time

EQUIPMENT

Two balls per student

DESCRIPTION

1. Have players get two balls each and scatter throughout the gym. Instruct them to hold one ball on each hand, palms up. Then have them dribble once and return the balls to the starting position.

2. After doing this successfully three to five times, have them try to increase the number of successful consecutive dribbles. Once they get used to dribbling two balls, they can try to execute the following, more challenging dribbles with two balls:

   - Stationary dribbling (emphasize keeping head up and eyes looking forward; see photo *a* on page 35)
   - Control dribble (emphasize dribbling at or below knee height, dribbling both balls in rhythm and not in rhythm)
   - Power dribble (adding movement by sliding to the side in both directions)
   - Speed dribble (emphasize keeping both balls out front at waist height or above, then add movement—walking first, then jogging; see photo *b* on pae 35)
   - High-low (control dribble with one hand and speed dribble with the other hand, then switch hands)
   - Change of direction
     - Reverse pivot
     - Power dribble with left foot leading; pivot and right foot leads

- Change hands
  - One ball crosses in front of the other
  - One through the legs with one crossover
  - One behind the back and one crossover

Adapted with permission of Don Meyer, Northern State University.

Time	National Standards	Grades
4-6 minutes	1, 2, 5	3-5

OBJECTIVES

1. Practice dribbling while looking up
2. Practice various dribbling skills (see activity 9, Four-Call Dribbling)
3. Compete in a gamelike activity

EQUIPMENT

One ball per student

DESCRIPTION

1. Have students partner up according to size and ability. Explain to them that they are going to have a "staring contest."
2. Instruct students to face their partner and look into each other's eyes (heads up) while dribbling in place. Any student who loses control, blinks, or looks away must begin again; that student's partner scores a point.

VARIATIONS

- To increase the challenge, time students and see which pairs can keep looking up the longest without losing control. After a few minutes with the first partner, give a signal at which students find another partner and begin the game again.

- If any pairs are executing the drill very successfully, challenge them to move either to the left, right, forward, or backward (all while still facing each other; one partner leads) while looking up.

- For older players (grades five and six), include two-ball dribbling (see activity 13) or four-call dribbling skills (activity 9).

Author: Shawn Fortner; used by permission of PE Central (www.pecentral.org), the premier Web site for physical educators.

Dribbling and Juggling 14

Time	National Standards	Grades
5-7 minutes	1, 2	4-6

OBJECTIVES

1. Develop dribbling skills, particularly with the weak hand
2. Improve ability to dribble without looking at the ball
3. Develop ability to divide attention among more than one task at a time

EQUIPMENT

One basketball, scarf, beanbag, and tennis ball per person

DESCRIPTION

1. Have students scatter throughout the space. Each student should have a basketball, a scarf, a beanbag, and a tennis ball. Begin with the scarf, placing the beanbag and tennis ball along the wall for safety.
2. Instruct students to dribble the basketball with their nondominant hand and juggle (toss and catch) the scarf with the strong hand. Begin juggling with a scarf because it floats slowly, then move on to a beanbag and last to a tennis ball.

VARIATIONS

For added challenge, have students toss the scarf, beanbag, or tennis ball using these variations:

- Increasingly higher
- Toss and catch behind the back
- Toss and catch with a partner (first underhand, then overhand as skills progress)
- Toss and catch a tennis ball or basketball with a partner while dribbling with the nondominant hand (emphasize moving the feet and then catching the ball with your eyes first and hand[s] second)

Adapted with permission of Don Meyer, Northern State University.

Time	National Standards	Grades
4-6 minutes	1, 2, 5, 6	K-2 (may be modified for grade 3-6 students)

OBJECTIVES

1. Practice simple dribbling and ball-handling skills
2. Warm up the body and practice skill repetitions in a semi-dynamic setting (performing an individual activity within a teacher-directed routine)
3. Explore spacing and working in a responsible manner in one's own space
4. Respond and listen to instructions
5. Learn to observe the floor and make decisions and adjustments on the go while executing the skills

EQUIPMENT

One basketball and hula hoop for each student; timed music (20 seconds of music with 10 seconds of silence or 30/30 or as suits variations to this activity)

DESCRIPTION

1. Instruct students to place a hula hoop on the floor, leaving a good amount of space between themselves and their classmates.
2. Have students begin dribbling between the hoops throughout the space using correct dribbling techniques. Instruct students to freeze and find the nearest hoop where they will do one of the activities suggested next.
3. About every 10 to 30 seconds, give a verbal signal to change the activity. Following is a list of various cues that the coach may use to provide increasingly more complex challenges to the students. If you are using timed music, have the students dribble (as described in the second step) while the music is

on. When the music stops, instruct them to find the nearest hoop to do the activity you will demonstrate. When the music begins, students resume dribbling between hoops.

a. Stationary activities

- Stand in a hoop and dribble with your right hand around the outside of the hoop (see photo *a* on page 40). Switch to your left hand and go the other direction. (Students should only dribble in either direction for about 10 seconds or less to avoid dizziness.)
- In-and-out double-single dribbles: Stand outside facing the hoop. Dribble the ball with the same hand twice inside the hoop and then twice outside the hoop. When ready, do single dribbles. Switch hands and repeat.
- Crossover dribble: Facing hoop, dribble twice outside the hoop (right hand), in the hoop once, then switch hands and dribble twice outside the hoop (left hand). (See photo *b* on page 41.) Now reverse directions without interruption. (Another pattern to try is single dribbles out, in, and out again.)
- Stand in the center of the hoop and spread your feet out until they both touch the opposite sides of the hoop. Dribble around the perimeter of the hoop, changing hands when necessary. Change directions.
- Stand in the hoop with feet staggered forward and back. Dribble twice outside the hoop, then go through the legs and dribble twice outside the hoop on the other side. Switch feet and repeat from the other direction.

b. Moving activities

- Using one of the four-call dribble skills (power, control, speed, and backup), kids move throughout the space. Emphasize keeping the head up and moving safely between the hoops. On a call or on their own timing, they perform a challenge (for example, dribble three times in a hoop, backup dribble into and out of a hoop, crossover into and out of a hoop, circle hoop).
- Dribble tag: Assign three children to be "it" and to try to tag or touch their classmates. The rest of the

class moves through the hoops. The hoops become safe zones if the children dribble their ball into a hoop (they can only dribble inside the hoop a maximum of five dribbles).

- Make patterns with multiple hoops and require dribbling through the hoops in a variety of patterns, such as a straight line or a circle. Use multiple dribbles in some hoops and single dribbles in others as appropriate. Creating signs to help students understand and remember the pattern is helpful.

a

b

TEACHING TIPS

- This activity can be used to develop skills. Once students are familiar with the activity, it can be used as a warm-up or as a skill–fitness activity.
- Direct all students to find a hoop quickly and freeze. Then, quickly model all skills from the perimeter, where all students can see you, and then get them going again with minimal delay. Quick teacher modeling allows for maximum repetitions and greater refinement of the desired skills.
- When adding movement to this activity, reinforce the importance of working safely in one's own space and controlling one's own body.
- Reinforce the importance of using the entire space.

16 Triangle Footwork

Time	National Standards	Grades
5-7 minutes	1, 2, 5, 6	3-6

OBJECTIVES

1. Practice three specific footwork patterns (slide, sprint, and backpedal)
2. Practice quick changes in direction
3. Develop sports-related fitness components of agility, speed, and balance

EQUIPMENT

Four to six balls for offensive footwork, none for defensive footwork

DESCRIPTION

1. Assign evenly matched partners and have each partner place his or her inside foot on the lane line.
2. On your "Go!" each partner slides toward the corner of the court. Instruct students to be sure to keep their hips square. When they reach the corner they plant the outside foot on the sideline, and redirect the inside foot toward the elbow (corner of lane line and free-throw line).
3. Next, students sprint to the elbow. Emphasize making a straight-line sprint to the elbow and not a banana curve. As they approach the elbow, they pound their feet to lower the center of gravity and ready themselves for the backpedal. Backpedaling is using a sprinting position to run backwards with shoulders over the toes.
4. Students backpedal down the lane line to the baseline. Reinforce moving safely by telling them to be sure that their shoulders are forward over their feet so that they do not lose their balance and fall backward.

Add a ball and turn this into an offensive drill(s) as follows:

- Power dribble to the sideline, speed dribble to the elbow, and backup dribble to the baseline.
- Pass the ball to the coach at the elbow, slide to the corner, and receive a pass in return. Pass again to the coach, sprint to the elbow, and establish a high-post (area on or near the free-throw line) position. The coach then passes the ball to the player who uses a power dribble to back down the lane and execute a post move and shot (such as a turnaround jump shot or a shot fake and drive).

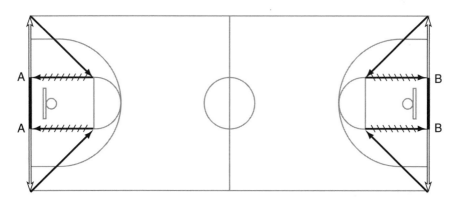

TEACHING TIPS

- Begin to prepare students for game pressure by first teaching this drill at half-speed; when the footwork is correct, increase speed and add competition, by racing or scoring, between partners.
- Remember to match size and speed for competition.
- Introduce more difficult skills only when footwork is proficient.

17 Clone Dribbling

Time	National Standards	Grades
5-7 minutes	1, 2, 5	5-6

OBJECTIVES

1. Practice dribbling while viewing the skills of another player
2. Execute skills sequentially

EQUIPMENT

One ball per person

DESCRIPTION

1. Partners begin with a control dribble facing each other cross-court.
2. On your signal, they advance toward the center of the court with a power or speed dribble. When they arrive, they resume control dribble, execute a change-of-direction skill (such as a crossover, reverse pivot, behind the back, or the like), and proceed to the opposite side from which they started.
3. Call out the type of dribble and the change-of-direction skill to be executed. A typical call for one rotation might sound like this: "Power, reverse pivot, and speed. Go!" Using the right hand, the partners would then advance using power dribble; once they arrive at center court they plant their front foot, execute a reverse pivot, and explode past their partner with a speed dribble.
4. Once players arrive at the opposite sideline, they go back to a control dribble.
5. On the next signal, they return using the left hand. Give students another three calls for the next down-and-back rotation.

Possible down-and-back rotation combinations include the following (add your own to this list):

- Power, reverse pivot, speed
- Power, crossover, speed

- Speed, behind the back, speed
- Power, through the legs, speed
- Speed, reverse pivot, speed
- Power, hesitate, speed
- Power, backup, speed

TEACHING TIP

Teach players to explode with a speed dribble following a change of direction or pace.

Adapted with permission of Don Meyer, Northern State University.

CHAPTER 4

PASSING

Learning to pass well is important for one reason: You can move the ball faster with a pass than with a dribble. This point was made clear to my students struggling with this concept in one of my practices. I asked the fastest player on the team to sprint to the far end of the gym from the baseline. When he got to half-court, I threw the ball off the far wall before he got to the far free-throw line. Thus, moving the ball with a pass is much more effective, because it is faster than the defense can run. Learning these skills to pass, as well as strengthening the muscles to do so, is critical to the game. These drills accomplish both in a fun, engaging, and challenging way.

18 Five Passes

Time	National Standards	Grades
2-3 minutes per game	1, 2, 5, 6	K-6

OBJECTIVES

1. Practice basketball-specific passing skills, pivoting, and defensive positioning
2. Compete as part of a team effort
3. Develop an understanding of basic basketball strategies and rules

EQUIPMENT

One or two basketballs, jerseys for one or two of the teams

DESCRIPTION

This activity is a fast-paced passing game that focuses on the successful completion of passes. This is a good drill to teach passing concepts (such as proper spacing, defensive position, and open passing lanes) before passing technique.

1. Divide the class into two even teams. One team wears jerseys.
2. Explain that the object of this game is for each team to complete five passes in a row in order to score a point. If the ball is dropped or intercepted, the other team begins its attempt to make five passes.
3. Begin by giving the ball to one team and say, "Go!"
4. Scoring: Keep track of the number of passes completed and when five is reached, play is stopped and a point is awarded. The ball is given to the other team and the game resumes. The game is over when either a certain number of points are earned or a certain amount of time (for example, 5 minutes) has passed.

VARIATIONS

- Begin with no restrictions on traveling.
- As players gain confidence, add restrictions of traveling and the use of a pivot foot.

- Add defensive positioning of an arm's length and no fouls.
- Add moving to open up passing lanes using a give-and-go strategy where a player passes the ball and moves to another spot to receive the ball back.
- Award a point only if five different team members receive passes.
- Award a point only if three different types of passes are used (you may specify types of passes or allow students to come up with their own).
- Add a 5-second count.
- A team may score after completing five passes.

TEACHING TIP

It is best to give minimal instructions to get this game started and add variations to it after each point is scored.

Adapted with permission from Bob Pangrazi.

Time	National Standards	Grades
10-20 minutes	1, 2, 5, 6	3-6

OBJECTIVES

1. Build passing and receiving skills
2. Learn a variety of passes
3. Work with a partner toward a common goal

EQUIPMENT

One ball per person

DESCRIPTION

Two-ball passing drills maximize practice efficiency while teaching players to pay attention to more than one thing at a time. Begin the drill by lining partners up opposite one another across the lane lines. Teach students the following progression of passes:

1. Chest Pass (one ball)

   Hold the ball at chest level with your fingers spread around it and your thumbs on top of it. Keep your elbows out and wide. Step to your target with either foot and throw the ball toward your partner's chest. Snap your thumbs down and through, fully extending your arms as you follow through. Use both hands equally. Higher-level skills include receiving the ball while it is in the air and passing off of each foot every other time (see photo *a* on page 51).

2. Chest-Bounce Pass (one ball)

   Execute a chest pass, except instead of aiming at your partner's chest, aim at a spot on the floor two-thirds of the distance between you and your partner. The ball should bounce up to your partner's waist height (see photo *b* on page 51).

3. Overs and Unders (two balls)

   One partner executes a chest pass (overs), and the other partner simultaneously executes a chest-bounce pass (unders; see photo *c* on page 52).

4. Push Pass (one ball)

Hold the ball in a shooting position over the right pocket (for right-handers): Place the right hand behind the ball, hold the wrist at 90 degrees, and place the left hand on the side of the ball for control and balance. Step with the same-side foot and shoot a pass to the left shoulder of your partner. The left hand should provide support and guidance but should not be used to make the pass (just like in shooting). Instead, use the left hand to give your partner a target. As soon as the pass is released, face your palm to your partner in front of your left shoulder for returning the pass (see photo *d* on page 52). (Cue the reverse for left-handers.)

a

b

c

d

5. Push Pass (two balls)

Both partners simultaneously execute a push pass, causing the balls to pass side by side. Higher-level skills include receiving the ball in the air, coming down on the back foot, and stepping immediately with the same-side foot to initiate the next pass.

VARIATION

Add a shot or pass fake before executing each pass.

Time	National Standards	Grades
5-10 minutes	1, 2, 5, 7	5-6

OBJECTIVES

1. Competing as part of a team effort
2. Engaging physical and mental skills simultaneously

EQUIPMENT

Two balls per group

DESCRIPTION

Teaching kids to process cognitive information while performing skills is valuable in helping them to think on the go. This activity combines the physical skills of passing, the use of one's peripheral vision, and thinking challenges.

1. Form each squad in a choir position (members standing side by side along a line with a leader facing the group) or in a circle with a leader in the center of the circle.

2. The leader holds one ball, and a player on his or her team holds another ball. The leader passes the ball to a different player and receives a pass from the player who held a ball. In this fashion the leader can go "down and back" or around the circle and then a new leader takes over. Once this pattern is learned, a variety of thinking challenges can be added.

   - The leader calls out each squad member's name as he or she passes the ball to the person.
   - Each member calls out the leader's name as each passes the ball to the leader.
   - Players call out numbers; state names; and basketball terms, plays, or aspects of the game that you choose for them to emphasize.
   - Use a variety of passes.

21 **Pass-and-Duck Relay**

Time	National Standards	Grades
5-8 minutes	1, 2, 5, 6	5-6

OBJECTIVES

1. Compete as a team toward achieving a common goal
2. Focus on using a variety of passing and dribbling skills

EQUIPMENT

One ball for each team

DESCRIPTION

1. Divide students into squads of four to six players and have them stand in open-squad formation (on evenly spaced lines from one baseline to the other; K-4 players may go from the baseline to the half-court line). Designate a leader for each team and give him or her a basketball.

2. On your signal, the leader passes to the first squad member, who passes it back and then ducks down and remains in the ducked position. The leader passes to the next person, who returns the pass and ducks. This sequence is repeated until the last person in the squad receives the pass. Upon receiving this pass, the last person in line runs to the front and all squad members move back one position. The drill is repeated until all squad members are back in their original positions.

3. Once the squad is back in its starting position, everyone sits down to signal that they are done. The team that is seated first wins.

4. If a ball is dropped due to a bad pass or fumble, this is a turnover that results in the ball returning to the leader, who must begin again.

VARIATIONS

- Use the same type of pass (chest, push, bounce, baseball, and so on) the entire time.

- Use a different type of pass depending on distance (for example, progressing from a bounce pass to a push pass to a chest pass to a baseball pass as the distance becomes greater).
- Use shorter distances (perhaps to half-court) and pass with the nondominant hand.
- Execute a layup following the speed dribble to the front (see activity 28).

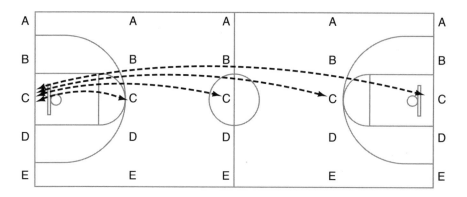

22 | Cannon Shot

Time	National Standards	Grades
7-10 minutes	1, 2, 5, 6	5-6

OBJECTIVES

1. Practice long-range, last-second shots
2. Practice the baseball pass to run the break
3. Learn to follow the pass or shot down the floor (to prepare for a rebound and the chance for a put-back)
4. Experience a game situation with time running out

EQUIPMENT

Two balls per team

DESCRIPTION

1. Line two teams up on opposite baselines. One team member is positioned at half-court and another at the far basket.

2. The first player in line on each team tosses the ball onto the backboard to start the game. The rebound is pulled off the backboard and a baseball outlet pass (first pass to start a fast break) is thrown to the player at half-court.

3. With no more than one dribble, this player must turn and shoot the ball at the basket. He or she can use a chest pass; a baseball pass; or, if the person has the strength, shoot the ball. The player at the far basket rebounds and dribbles the ball back to the opposite end and joins his or her team.

VARIATIONS

- Modify this activity to create shots from any particular place on the floor or in combination with an out-of-bounds play.
- Add more dribbles for younger players to get closer to the basket (but realize that more dribbles take more time).

- Teams can compete against one another or compete together as part of a team effort.
- Switch sides of the floor so that players practice shooting from both sides of the floor.

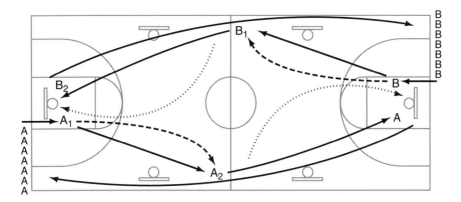

Time	National Standards	Grades
4-6 minutes	1, 2	5-6

OBJECTIVES

1. Accomplish a skill–fitness routine
2. Build the motor patterns and muscle endurance needed for making passes
3. Strengthen heart and lung endurance
4. Develop footwork patterns specific to the game of basketball

EQUIPMENT

One ball per partnership

DESCRIPTION

1. Partners stand front to back facing a wall at a distance of 8 to 10 feet (about 2 to 3 meters).
2. The front partner executes a chest pass to the wall and immediately slides to the side, then behind his or her partner (see photo on page 59). The back partner receives the pass and repeats the process. The partners try to get into a rhythm of sliding to the side and back again, circling one another while keeping the ball in motion.

TEACHING TIPS

- Go in one direction and then switch.
- Use a variety of passes such as chest, chest-bounce, overhead, and right-handed or left-handed push passes.
- Go for 20 seconds to 30 seconds at a time and then change directions or pass type. Give the players a 10- to 20-second rest period between bouts. This activity is highly intense, and it will provide a great workout while students are practicing skills.

CHAPTER 5

SHOOTING

Shooting is not easy to learn. Many different types of shots (layups, free throws, set-shots, jump shots, and so on) must be learned. Then these shots must be executed in very difficult and ever-changing game situations. These activities are intended to help students learn to shoot a variety of shots in a variety of ways. Some drills provide maximum repetitions while others are more gamelike and competitive. Remind players that shooting the ball into the hoop is only one measure of success when learning to shoot properly. Proper form and execution are more important for young players; missing a shot is just part of the game. Too often, young players use improper technique because they lack the strength or skill to perform a shot correctly. Help players by starting them close to the basket, using smaller balls, lowering baskets, and using different targets (e.g., lines or hoops on the floor) to focus on proper technique before trying gamelike situations.

Time	National Standards	Grades
3-5 minutes per game	1, 2, 5, 6	4-6

OBJECTIVES

1. Practice shooting from a variety of spots on the floor
2. Practice following one's own shot
3. Practice rebounding and putting the ball back in the hoop
4. Experience competition in a game situation

EQUIPMENT

Five poly spots at each basket; one ball per team

DESCRIPTION

Twenty-One is a competitive game that simulates game situations where moving quickly, anticipating the direction of a rebound, and shooting a high percentage can make the difference between winning and losing.

1. Explain to the class that they will play a game whose object is to be the first team to score 21 points. A shot made from the poly spot is worth 2 points. If they miss they can get the rebound and make a layup for 1 point.
2. Divide the class into teams of three to five players, and position them facing the basket in a single-file line behind spot 1 (see diagram). Instruct them to begin on your go signal.
3. Teams call out their score each time point(s) are scored so that everyone can hear.
4. The game is over when the first team reaches 21 points.
5. Repeat at spot 2 and so on.

VARIATIONS

- For grades five and six, a layup can be attempted only if the rebound is caught before hitting the ground. This method teaches them to follow their shot.

- One of the five spots can be at the free-throw line, but scoring is all by 1 point for each made free throw and no layups are allowed.
- Choose any configuration of spots that suits the particular needs of your class.

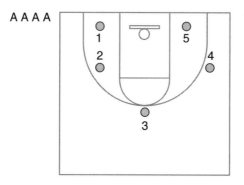

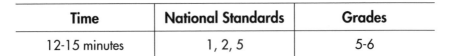

25 Basketball Golf

Time	National Standards	Grades
12-15 minutes	1, 2, 5	5-6

OBJECTIVES

1. Practice shooting from a variety of spots on the floor
2. Engage in competition

EQUIPMENT

One ball, scorecard, and pencil for each student; signs for each basket

DESCRIPTION

1. Set up six shooting stations in the form of a golf course, with a station at each basket.
2. Prepare scorecards similar to a golf scorecard, with a square for each of the team members and each of the six holes (baskets, see diagram). A brief description and par for each hole should be listed.
3. Divide your class evenly into six teams, and send one team to each of the six stations. Explain that they will play a shooting game similar to golf and that there are signs at each basket explaining what to do. Tell them that all teams will begin simultaneously and that each player will record his or her score following each basket. Remind students that the lower the score, the better.
4. If competition is the goal, the player with the low score wins. If not, then personal goals can be the focus and students can keep track of their best score and try to do better each time.

VARIATION

The additional challenge of making certain shots count only if they are "nothing but net" may be used for players with greater ability.

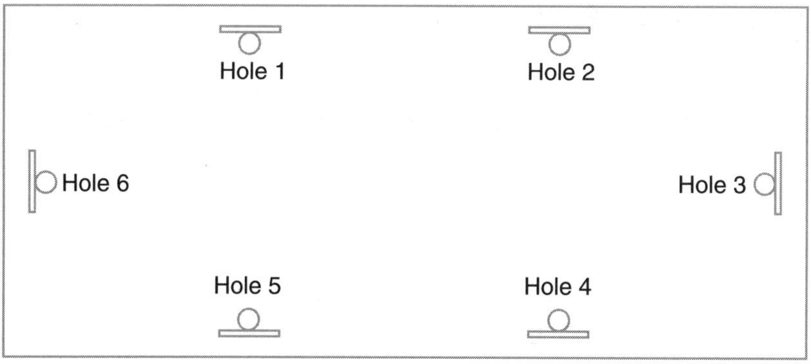

Hole 1

Hole 2

Hole 6

Hole 3

Hole 5

Hole 4

Hole 1 Par 3	Hole 2 Par 4	Hole 3 Par 3	Hole 4 Par 5	Hole 5 Par 4	Hole 6 Par 3
2 right-handed layups	2 left-handed layups	2 free throws	2 three pointers	3 jump shots from the wing	1 shot from each block
Score:	Score:	Score:	Score:	Score:	Score:
				Total:	

Time	National Standards	Grades
12-15 minutes	1, 2, 5	5-6

OBJECTIVES

1. Compete as an individual or as a team while working toward a common goal
2. Focus on three essential shooting skills: free throw, layup, and three point
3. Accomplish a skill–fitness routine

EQUIPMENT

Balls, stopwatches, cones

DESCRIPTION

1. Arrange students into groups of three. Explain that they will compete as a team in a triathlon with each team member performing one of the following activities: (a) Free-throw shooting, (b) layup shooting, and (c) inside–outside shooting.

2. Leg 1. Free throws: One player shoots 25 free throws while a partner/scorer rebounds, counts, and tosses the ball back to the shooter. The score is how many were made out of 25. Repeat until each team member completes the leg. The team score is the total shots made out of 75.

3. Leg 2. Layups: A player starting outside the three-point line shoots 10 right-handed and 10 left-handed layups each with no more than three dribbles inside the three-point line. One point is earned for each layup made with three dribbles, 2 points for two dribbles, and 3 points for one dribble inside the three-point line. Repeat until all team members have completed the leg. The team score is the total amount of points for all 3 members.

4. Leg 3. Inside–outside shooting: Poly spots are laid out as shown in the diagram. The shooter can choose whichever spots (1, 2, or 3 pointers) he or she wishes to attempt. There is a 3-minute time limit in which the shooter makes as many shots

as possible. The shooter retrieves his or her own rebound and goes to a new spot each time. Explain to students that strategy is important: The closer shots are easier but score fewer points. A long rebound might be a good chance to shoot a three pointer. Repeat until all of the team members have completed the leg. The team score is the total amount of points from all the members. Timed music of 1 minute will make the third leg (inside–outside shooting) more exciting and make management easier and more consistent.

5. Add up the scores from each of the three team members. High score wins.

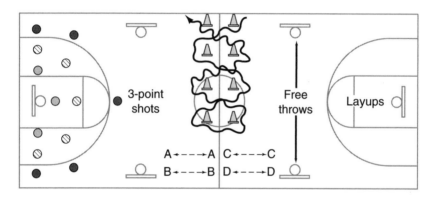

- Change the events to focus on any particular skill(s) as needed.
- Hold competitions for individuals or groups of three students.
- Hold events over three consecutive days to allow students to develop strategies, or all activities can be done the same day.
- To increase difficulty, create a basketball pentathlon (five events). Add the following two legs to the triathlon:
  - Push passes: With a partner and one or two balls, students complete as many right-handed push passes across the width of the lane as they can in 30 seconds. If one ball is used, 1 point is awarded for each successful pass. If two balls are used, 2 points are awarded for each successful pass.
  - Dribble through the cones: Students dribble through eight cones each with a ball on top. This event is timed. Use a stopwatch to time the attempt and then total up the team members' times. The fastest time earns 100 points, next fastest earns 90, and so on. Each ball that is knocked off results in a 2-second penalty.

TEACHING TIP

When done as a team the basketball triathlon points out that everyone has certain strengths and can contribute to the team by filling a role that matches her or his strength(s).

Time	National Standards	Grades
3-5 minutes per game	1, 2	3-6

OBJECTIVES

1. Explore gamelike pressure while focusing on shooting, rebounding, and layups
2. Practice following the shot
3. Practice rebounding and put-backs

EQUIPMENT

Two balls per group

DESCRIPTION

1. Players line up at the free-throw line, in single file, facing the basket.

2. The first two players in line each hold a ball. The first player in line shoots the ball. The second player cannot shoot until the ball is out of the hand of the first player. If the player in front makes the shot, he or she gives the ball to the next person in line and then goes to the end of the line. If the shooter misses, he or she rebounds and shoots until the shot is made. If, however, a player cannot make a shot before the next player makes his or her shot, the player who is missing shots is eliminated. The last player in the game wins.

3. To play again, students line up in reverse order of how they were eliminated. Plan some ball-handling drills for players to work on once they are eliminated and are waiting for the game to be completed. Keep the squads small so that each player gets to shoot as much as possible.

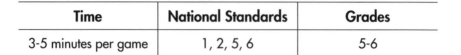

Time	National Standards	Grades
3-5 minutes per game	1, 2, 5, 6	5-6

OBJECTIVES

1. Experience head-to-head competition in a shooting game
2. Shoot from the outside from increasing distances

EQUIPMENT

One ball per person

DESCRIPTION

1. Match players with a partner. Send equal numbers of partnerships to each of the six baskets.
2. Partners begin facing the hoop from below the block on the lane line. On your signal, each partner attempts a shot from that spot and retrieves his or her own rebound. If the player makes the shot, he or she moves to the next spot up the lane (see diagram) and shoots again. If the player misses the shot, he or she must remain on the same spot until the shot is made. The first player to make the last shot at the elbow wins. These are short and intense games; thus it is important to have the other players ready to go for their turn by waiting under the basket.

VARIATIONS

- The player moves back to the starting spot if he or she misses a shot.
- Players shoot around the horn (travel up the lane, shoot a free throw, and continue down the other side).

TEACHING TIP

Remind players to follow their shots, rebound cleanly from the perimeter, and square up to the basket after coming from the inside.

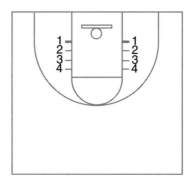

29 Layup Circuit

Time	National Standards	Grades
9-12 minutes	1, 2	5-6

OBJECTIVES

1. Shoot a variety of layup shots
2. Practice independently
3. Learn to shoot and dribble with both the left and right hands

EQUIPMENT

One ball per player, timed music (90 seconds of music with 15 seconds of silence)

DESCRIPTION

1. In advance of this activity, prepare a sign or poster that explains the type of layup to be done at each of the six stations (baskets). Assign students to one of each of the six baskets.

2. Students perform the layup shots while the music is playing, doing as many of that particular type as they can, and then rotate clockwise to the next basket during the silence. The following is a list of possible layup shots (feel free to add your own):

   • Right-handed layups: Jump off the left foot, raise the right knee and hand, and shoot the ball high and soft off the top right-hand corner of the square.

   • Left-handed layups: Jump off the right foot, raise the left knee and hand, and shoot the ball high and soft off the top right-hand corner of the square.

   • Drop-step layups: Start with the back to the basket on the low-post block; step with foot lowest to baseline, turning the toe toward the basket; and shoot the ball high and soft off the near side top corner of the square. Players should alternate blocks.

   • Fewer-dribbles layups: Start beyond the three-point line and shoot a layup with three dribbles or less inside the three-point line, trying to use as few dribbles inside the three-point line as possible.

- Give-and-go layups: Pass the ball to a partner and cut to the basket, receive the ball in stride, and shoot the layup without a dribble.

- Your-choice layups: Students do whatever kind of layup they wish. Suggest that kids be creative (go around your back, through your legs, behind your left ear).

Time	National Standards	Grades
3-5 minutes	1, 2, 5, 6	5-6

OBJECTIVES

1. Learn to be a successful competitor while working as a team
2. Focus on shooting skills
3. Concentrate on ball-handling skills: dribbling with the weak hand, speed and control dribbles

EQUIPMENT

One ball for each player

DESCRIPTION

1. Set players up in squad formation on the baseline. Squad members cheer each other on while dribbling in place with their weak hand.

2. The first player speed dribbles to one of the three baskets in the opposite end of the court and shoots until he or she makes a free throw. Each time the first player makes a free throw, the next player in line can advance using a speed dribble and executing a jump stop into control dribble position, first to the near free-throw line extended, then to the half-court, and last to the far free-throw line extended.

3. On the fourth free throw made by the first player, the next advancing player joins the leader and begins to shoot free throws. Now there are two shooters to bring squad members across. When the two shooters make the fourth free throw there are now three shooters to bring the next squad member across, and so on. Shooters can best move their squad members across by making a high percentage of shots but also by hustling for rebounds on a missed shot and returning quickly to the free-throw line to shoot again.

4. The team who has all squad members at the free-throw line first must then have each member make a free throw to win the game. Each member must retrieve his or her own rebound.

- Encourage students to set up a shot with good balance and to be quick but still execute the shot correctly.
- Remind students that following one's shot is the key to success in this activity so that no time is wasted between shots.

CHAPTER 6

MULTISKILL ACTIVITIES

In most classrooms and practice sessions, there are more students who need attention than there are teachers and coaches who can give the attention to them. Thus, it is important to build good work habits in the students so that they learn to become self-directed in their learning activities. The activities in this chapter provide increased levels of self-directed learning within a structured activity; they also provide the students with maximum skill-building repetitions as they address a variety of basketball skills presented in a fun and engaging way.

Time	National Standards	Grades
12-15 minutes	1, 2, 5, 6	4-6

OBJECTIVES

1. Practice a variety of basketball skills including passing, shooting, and ball handling
2. Make self-directed choices about what skills to practice

EQUIPMENT

One basketball, hoops playing card, and pencil per student; 8 cones; signs for stations

DESCRIPTION

1. In advance, place cones and signs out for the activities as needed, assuring safety and ease of transition.
2. Pass out a hoops playing card, with various skills listed in each square (see page 79), and a pencil to each student.
3. Explain to your students that they will play a game that is similar to bingo, only their playing cards will have the word "hoops" at the top of each column instead of the word "bingo."
4. Students must complete each assignment in the square before marking it off. To win the game students must make a horizontal line, x, diagonal, or a blackout. This activity can be carried out over several days to ensure that students practice all of the skills listed. Students make choices and practice simple strategies to completing the game.

TEACHING TIPS

- Move throughout the crowd assessing and giving feedback and encouragement where needed.
- Making and posting the signs and cards beforehand will decrease the amount of instructional time and increase the self-direction skills of the players. Creating a simple table in a word processor format allows you to easily customize the skills

H	O	O	P	S
Dribble the basketball 10 times while standing still	Chest-bounce pass the ball 20 times to a partner, standing 15 feet apart	With both hands, bounce the ball back through your knees and catch it 3 times	Do a right-handed layup 3 times using correct form	Dribble (using your weaker hand) around all three circles while walking
Make 15 chest passes to a partner or to the wall	Dribble through the cones using your strong hand	Shoot 3 shots from outside of the lane	Ball handling: Do 5 figure-8 patterns around your knees	Shoot 3 shots from inside of the lane and in front of the basket
Shoot 2 shots from each block using the backboard	Ball handling: Move the ball around your waist 5 times in each direction	Free	Bounce pass to a partner who turns and shoots 3 times	Ball handling: Move ball around knees 5 times in each direction
Dribble around all 3 circles, while jogging and using your strong hand	Shoot 3 free throws using correct form	Dribble the ball in place 15 times with each hand	Pass in a zig-zag pattern to a partner, doing 10 of both chest passes and bounce passes	Make 3 baseball passes to a partner who is down one sideline
Perform a give-and-go pass and shot with a partner 3 times	Dribble around the court perimeter lines one time with each hand	Dribble between your legs 3 times	Make a chest pass to the wall, dribble to opposite basket, and shoot a layup	Shoot 3 one-handed jump shots

for each session, so that you can create your own progression to suit the specific needs of your class or team. Try working on specific themes such as defensive skills, shooting, ball handling, or general skills (similar to those suggested in the diagram).

- Change the level of difficulty for increased age and ability.
- Students can complete a blackout if time allows. A blackout ensures that each student practices all of the assigned skills.

Adapted with permission from Lois Mauch.

Time	National Standards	Grades
10-15 minutes	1, 2, 3	3-6

OBJECTIVES

1. Practice a variety of basketball-specific skills
2. Develop self-directed learning skills

EQUIPMENT

One ball per student, station signs, scavenger-hunt cards

DESCRIPTION

As with all scavenger hunts, the students scavenge a list in this game—in this case, a list of basketball skills. This activity allows the teacher or coach to address a variety of skills in a gamelike competitive activity that is still a great deal of fun for kids.

1. Create in advance a set of cards (one for every team) listing 10 to 15 basketball skills. Some suggested skills are listed later in this activity. Each card will list the same skills, but in varying order, to ensure that this drill is a small-group pursuit, not just a large-group activity.
2. Divide the students into teams of four to six players.
3. Give a card to each team and explain that they are to scavenge each of the items listed by completing the tasks. The first team to fully complete all items wins.
4. Listed next are some possible items for the scavenger hunt. Feel free to design and include any others that you feel meet your students' needs.
   - 10 give-and-go layups
   - 30 consecutive right-handed and left-handed push passes using two balls simultaneously
   - 30 partner wall passes while rotating front to back (see activity 23)
   - 5 no-rim (nothing but net) jump or set shots from the blocks

- Dribble through the cones
- 5 left-handed layups with correct form (jumping off of the right foot and shooting with the left hand)
- 5 right-handed layups with correct form (jumping off of the left foot and shooting with the right hand)
- 1 three-point shot from five spots around the arc (marked with poly spots; one on each baseline, one on each wing, and one at the top of the key)
- 3 "dribbling ladders": dribbling down the court with the right hand; then dribbling with the left hand on the way back
- 5 free throws

TEACHING TIP

A gamelike and competitive atmosphere is part of this activity. Consider awarding a prize of some kind as the groups complete the activity.

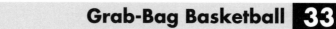

Time	National Standards	Grades
7-10 minutes	1, 2, 5, 6	5-6 (can be modified for students K-4)

OBJECTIVES

1. Repeat and refine previously learned skills
2. Engage in self-directed forms of learning activities
3. Explore spacing and working in a responsible manner in one's own space while performing activities on the selected card
4. Practice self- and peer coaching in analyzing one's own performance

EQUIPMENT

4 buckets, boxes, hoops, or bags; index cards with individual skills and tasks described on each one

DESCRIPTION

The cards in this activity allow students to self-manage and remain on task individually, thus providing a greater number of skill-building repetitions than can be achieved in a more typical large-group drill.

1. Prepare many index cards listing a variety of skills and tasks to be performed related to the game of basketball. These activities can be intended for warm-up, skill, or even fitness purposes. Distribute the cards evenly among four grab-bag buckets placed in the corners of the gym.
2. Direct the students to go to one of the four grab bags on your go signal, retrieve a card, and follow the directions on the card. After executing the skill, they will go back to any one of the four grab bags, exchange cards, and perform the skill indicated on the card. Remind them that they must complete the activity on the card they have taken before exchanging it for another card.

- Use timed music (such as 30-40 seconds on and 15 seconds off) and have the students perform while the music is on and retrieve a new card when the music is off.
- For K-4 students, fill the grab bags with index cards numbered from 5 to 15 and direct them as follows:
  - Tell the students that on your go signal, each student will go to one of the four grab bags in the corners and retrieve a numbered card. Then they will return to their space on the floor and begin doing the number of left-handed dribbles indicated on the card. If they finish before everyone else, they should repeat the activity until you signal the class to stop.
  - Repeat the same instructions with a new activity such as right-handed dribbles, layups, dribbling through the legs, moving the ball around the waist, moving the ball through the legs, shooting free throws, passing against the wall, tossing and catching to self, and so on.
- K-4 students could also be offered up to three activities or choices of activities (for example, right-handed dribbles, tosses and catches, and wall passes). So, if students choose a card with the number "8," they would perform 8 right-handed dribbles, 8 tosses and catches, and 8 wall passes. If they finish early, have them repeat the activity until you signal the class to stop.
- You can also give students three skills choices and let them choose which of the three they want to do.

TEACHING TIPS

- Be sure to have a mix of activities that promote kids' enjoyment while building their skill and fitness.
- Model all skills that may be new for the younger students before they perform the skills themselves.
- Reinforce the importance of working safely in one's own space and controlling one's own ball and body.
- Reinforce the importance of using the entire space.
- Remind students to move to and from the grab bag quickly.

Horse for the Course 34

Time	National Standards	Grades
10-12 minutes	1, 2, 5	5-6

OBJECTIVES

1. Practice ball-handling and passing skills at game speed
2. Work to beat one's personal best
3. Experience competition and team play

EQUIPMENT

One ball for each student, signs for each basket, one stopwatch per group (or large clock), scorecards, cones, playground balls, tumbling mats

DESCRIPTION

1. This is a timed team event. Scoring is similar to an equestrian event, in which the score is kept in terms of time and number of faults while running the course. "Par" is a preset time with no faults. Because each course will vary in terms of space and configuration, you must establish par for your students. All teams try to complete the course in the least time with the fewest faults.

2. Have students form groups of four to six players. Give each group a stopwatch and scorecard. Position each team at one of the baskets. A sample obstacle course setup and scorecard are shown here (see figures on pages 86 and 87).

3. Explain the game to the students as follows: "This activity is like a horse race and relay combined. Each team member will attempt to complete the course as quickly as possible with the fewest mistakes, called faults. When I say, 'Go!' one person in the group will start the stopwatch, and it will run until the last team member has finished. While one person is running the course, team members replace equipment that may get knocked out of place. But, be careful not to get in another team's way. Another team member keeps track of the number of faults committed. When one team member finishes the

course, he or she hands the ball to the next team member who then begins. When all team members are done, the watch is stopped. Each fault adds 3 seconds to the total time. The team with the lowest resulting time wins."

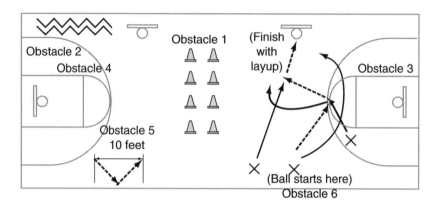

Obstacle 1	Obstacle 2	Obstacle 3	Obstacle 4	Obstacle 5	Obstacle 6
Dribble through 8 cones with balls on top	Power dribble through the mat maze	Shoot a free throw, get the rebound before it hits the floor, and put it in	Make two 3 pointers	Complete 15 wall passes to self, moving 10 feet side to side	A group of 3 completes five 3-man weaves with a layup
One fault for each ball knocked off	One fault for each time a ball or person touches the mats	One fault if the free throw or layup is missed. One fault if rebound touches floor	One fault for each miss. Earn back a fault if you get the rebound before it hits the ground	One fault for each dropped ball. One fault for each time the foot does not touch the sideline	One fault for a dropped pass, violation, or missed layup
Time:	Time:	Time:	Time:	Time:	Time:
Faults:	Faults:	Faults:	Faults:	Faults:	Faults:
Time:			Faults:		

35 Baton Relay

Time	National Standards	Grades
5-7 minutes	1, 2, 5, 6	3-6

OBJECTIVES

1. Compete as a team toward achieving a common goal
2. Focus on dribbling and shooting skills, especially the speed dribble and shooting layups at breakaway speed
3. Improve timing for making rebounds
4. Improve overall conditioning

EQUIPMENT

One ball for each squad

DESCRIPTION

1. Four-member squads compete in a tracklike event in which the baton (the ball) is moved around the track in the shortest possible time.
2. Place cones in an oval track around the volleyball court (see diagram). Use a staggered start (one squad at each of the six baskets), but everyone can move into the inside lane after the first curve.
3. Any fouls (for example, bumping into another player) cause a team to be disqualified.
4. One player from each team speed dribbles to complete two laps and returns to his or her starting basket. After completing two laps, the first squad member must shoot and make a layup. When the ball goes through, the second person rebounds the ball and begins taking his or her two laps. The first team to finish wins the relay race.

VARIATIONS

- Shorten or lengthen the race (try one or three laps instead of two).
- Shoot a layup at each of the six baskets in the gym.

- Take 3 seconds off the time if the rebound is taken before the ball hits the floor.
- For sixth graders, the "in-the-hole" player can rebound and throw an outlet pass to the "on-deck" player. Learning to clear the rebound and throw the outlet pass prepares students to master the first steps of the fast-break offense. Like a relay race, the outlet pass must be made within a passing zone, or a 5-second penalty is assessed. However, if the pass is made in stride it can greatly reduce the overall time.

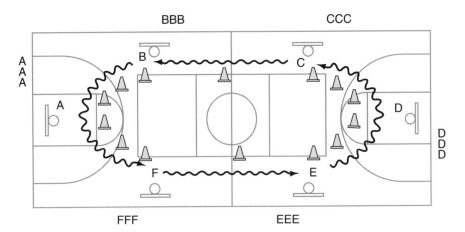

36 Pinwheel

Time	National Standards	Grades
7-12 minutes	1, 2, 5, 6	5-6

OBJECTIVES

1. Build skills needed for running the fast break
2. Move the ball down the entire length of the court by passing not dribbling
3. Compete for a team goal
4. Shoot layups at game speed

EQUIPMENT

Two balls

DESCRIPTION

This fast-moving, goal-oriented activity is a favorite of players and students alike; use the pinwheel to set the tone for an exciting class or practice. Students may need to run the drill a few times before they can do it well, but the repetition is worth the effort.

1. This drill is mirrored on both sides of the floor, but you should focus on one side only to be less confusing. Two players (one at each end) start this activity by tossing a ball off the backboard, rebounding it, and throwing an outlet pass to a player waiting on the wing.
2. The rebounders/passers then streak down the outside lane, receive the pass back from the outlet players, and continue down the floor passing and receiving the ball to players as indicated in the diagram. Use a chest pass or flip pass as needed.
3. After receiving the last pass, the two passers shoot a layup and then join the line as shown. Each player follows his or her pass to the next position and repeats the pattern with the next shooter.
4. After this drill is learned, time the group for 2 minutes to see how many layups they can make in that time.

For older or more skilled players, bad passes or fumbles negate the
layup. In other words, only clean runs count so that good passing
and receiving is emphasized. Run this drill to the right and to the
left side to practice layups on both sides.

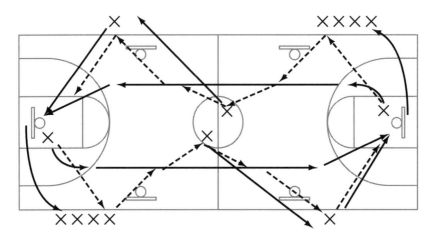

Time	National Standards	Grades
10-15 minutes	1, 2, 4, 6	3-6

OBJECTIVES

1. Practice a variety of basketball skills
2. Develop heart and lung fitness through continuous movement and multiple practice attempts

EQUIPMENT

Signs for each station, poly spots, cones, one basketball per student, music (7 to 8 minutes in length, age-appropriate, prepared in advance, continuous or interval), CD/tape player

DESCRIPTION

1. Set up a steeplechase course consisting of a variety of basketball skills around the perimeter of the gym. Any set of specific skills can be emphasized in the steeplechase course. Each skill should be continuous in nature and be accompanied by a sign that explains the activity.

2. Direct students to get a ball from the perimeter of the room and begin dribbling in their own space throughout the open middle of the gym.

3. Once they are evenly spaced, direct students to move to the nearest station and begin the activity as indicated on the station sign once the music begins. Direct all students to move in the same direction (either clockwise or counterclockwise). You can modify the stations to accomplish a variety of skill objectives. Here are some suggested station ideas (see accompanying diagram):

   - Dribble through cones using the right and left hands with a crossover dribble.
   - Make chest passes to the wall while sliding. Make at least three passes.
   - Speed dribble to the first cone, flip the feet out in front, and begin a control dribble; power dribble to the next

cone using the right hand, round the next cone, and power dribble to the subsequent cone using the left hand. Continue.

- Shoot a free throw.
- Make right-handed push passes to the wall while sliding. Make at least three passes.
- Dribble the ball inside each of the hoops and around two of the hoops.
- Shoot once from each of three poly spots.

VARIATION

Make music continuous to emphasize heart and lung fitness or alternate the music with intervals of silence to allow the inclusion of flexibility or strength exercises with or without the basketball.

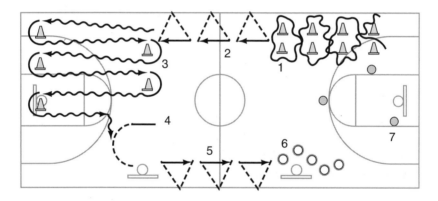

38 Racetrack

Time	National Standards	Grades
5-7 Minutes	1, 2, 4, 5, 6	3-6

OBJECTIVES

1. Practice a variety of basketball skills with maximum number of practice attempts
2. Strengthen heart and lung fitness through continuous movement
3. Develop ability to collaborate with a partner

EQUIPMENT

Signs for each station, one basketball per student, music (7 to 8 minutes in duration, age appropriate, prepared in advance, continuous or interval with 45 seconds of music interspersed with 15 seconds of silence), CD/tape player

DESCRIPTION

This routine takes advantage of the popularity of auto racing. It alternates aerobic activities with basketball skills activities. The aerobic activities take place on the "racetrack," and the basketball skills activities take place in the "pit."

1. Students choose a partner, one of whom goes to the center of the floor (the pit) to become part of the pit crew, and the other who goes to the perimeter of the gym (the racetrack) to become a driver.
2. While the music is on, the driver dribbles around the racetrack and the pit crew in the center performs basketball skills activities as indicated on signs located in the pit. Any set of specific skills can be worked on in the pit area. Prepare a sign for each skill that explains the activity.
3. When the music stops, the driver returns to the pit where the partners switch roles with a high-five. The new driver dribbles around the track while the new pit crew practices basketball skills.

VARIATIONS

- Make the music continuous, and direct the drivers to return to the pit after they have completed a predetermined number of laps.
- Change the shape of the racetrack (for example, try a figure 8), or place cones throughout the track to provide an added challenge.
- Add partner goals, challenges, and competition.

TEACHING TIP

This skill–fitness routine is particularly suited to the intermittent nature of children's activity patterns. By engaging in short, intense activities, children don't get bored or frustrated because they are learning to stay focused on a set of ever-changing tasks.

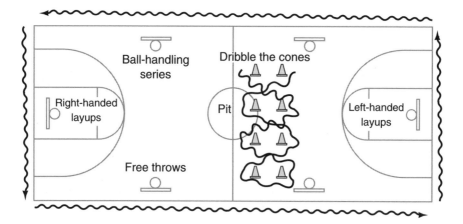

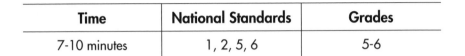

Time	National Standards	Grades
7-10 minutes	1, 2, 5, 6	5-6

OBJECTIVES

1. Practice components of the fast break: rebound, outlet pass, filling the post, entry pass, and layup
2. Strengthen basketball-specific skills and physical conditioning

EQUIPMENT

Two balls

DESCRIPTION

1. The post player tosses a ball off the backboard to start the drill. After the rebound is in the hands of the post player, the guard breaks toward half-court and calls, "Outlet, Outlet!" letting the post player know the guard is ready for a pass.

2. The post player throws the outlet pass and then sprints to the opposite end of the court and "fills the lane" (that is, he or she sprints to the elbow, pounds the feet, throws the hands up, and slides to the block ready to receive the pass from the guard). Simultaneously, the guard receives the outlet pass, pivots, dribbles to the wing three-point line, and executes a jump stop into triple-threat position (ball on hip and ready to drive, shoot, or pass). At this point the post player should be filling the post.

3. The guard makes an entry pass to the post player (work on a variety of passes such as the overhead, bounce, or chest pass) who then executes a post move (coach's choice or of the player's choosing such as a drop step or a fake and pivot) or passes the ball back out to the guard. Once the entry pass is made the guard moves to the corner ready to receive a pass back from the post and shoot the three-point shot. This activity is executed on both sides of the floor so a little competition or a team goal can be added.

TEACHING TIP

Not only is this activity an excellent conditioning drill, but it also develops fast-break skills and the ability to run the floor with a purpose. Each player has a specific objective (rebounding, outlet, filling the post, or spotting up) so that the fast break is not just an undisciplined rush down the court.

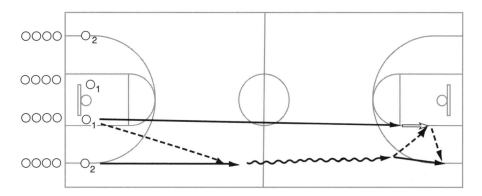

40   Four Corners

Time	National Standards	Grades
7-10 minutes	1, 2, 5, 6	6

OBJECTIVES

1. Practice a variety of sequentially linked skills
2. Practice moving at game speed
3. Work together as a team toward a common outcome and within a specific pattern

DESCRIPTION

This drill is a little more complicated but is an excellent drill to create team discipline and the ability to fill the role assigned to you. Be sure to look at the diagram while reading each point of the following description.

1. Four squads are located at the four corners of the half-court. Each squad is labeled in the diagram as A, B, C, and D. Rotate in reverse order from A to D to C to B to A following each cycle of the drill.
2. The ball starts in A, is passed (black-dotted arrows) to B to C and to D, then back to A (note red-arrow path) for a layup.
3. D gets the rebound and passes to B who is waiting at the free-throw line. B closes out (defends against) D. D can shoot from the free-throw line or drive. C makes one pass and rotates to D immediately so as to not get into the middle of the activity and cause confusion. After the shot the ball is cleared and the next group begins.

TEACHING TIPS

- Once the students learn this drill, be sure to run it at game speed. The ball should never touch the floor, resulting in a layup and a second shot under pressure. Assign the type of passes you want your students to work on in this drill. Have the students practice going in both directions. The goal is to make a certain percentage of the layups.

- Setting a goal for a certain percentage of the layups made (such as 7 out of 10, or 70%) is very beneficial. Motivate students even more by encouraging them to try to beat their previous scores.
- This activity is also an excellent pregame warm-up drill.

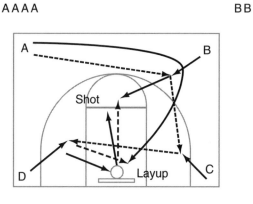

41 Challenge Basketball

Time	National Standards	Grades
10-15 minutes	1, 2, 5, 6	5-6

OBJECTIVES

1. Compete as part of a team while working toward a common goal
2. Practice and refine skills

EQUIPMENT

One ball for each court, 2 or more basketball courts (such as cross-court)

DESCRIPTION

Challenge basketball involves three on three (or fewer) play and engages students in nearly all of the basketball-specific skills in a gamelike activity. All players get to contribute, and the routine allows for quick and manageable rotation of larger groups.

1. Teams of three students each line up beneath one basket. The first two teams play out a point.
2. The team that scores remains on the floor to face the next challenger. The challenger team inbounds the ball and tries to defeat the reigning champions.
3. The object is to remain on the floor as long as possible.
4. Place restrictions or promotions on the games to encourage students to focus on one or more types of skills. Here are some examples of restrictions you might use:
   - Score with a layup only.
   - Score with an outside shot only.
   - Pass the ball into the key and then come out once before you can score.
   - Each player on a team has to handle the ball before anyone can take a shot.

- Once a player has shot the ball, the player must wait to shoot again until after the other team members have taken a shot.

Examples of promotions you might use include the following:

- Score 1 point for every teammate who touched the ball when the basket is made.
- Score 1 point for an outside shot.
- Score 2 points for a right-handed layup and 3 points for a left-handed layup.

5. Play one game for 5 minutes and change the restrictions or promotions.

VARIATION

Playing with reduced squads (one on one, two on two, and three on three) allows for more frequent application of the skills than do full-squad games.

42 Sideline Basketball

Time	National Standards	Grades
7-12 minutes	1, 2, 5, 6	4-6

OBJECTIVES

1. Focus on passing and receiving skills in a game situation
2. Develop team strategies

EQUIPMENT

Jerseys for half the class, one or two balls

DESCRIPTION

1. Split the entire class into two teams (or four teams if using two crosscourts). One team wears jerseys.
2. Each team lines up on one sideline of the basketball court. The first three-member squad from each team takes the floor. All other team members space themselves evenly along their sideline.
3. Regular three-on-three play begins, but before a team can score they must pass the ball to their sideline teammates at least three times, placing more emphasis on passing.
4. After each made basket (or two), rotate a new squad into the game. Rotating is accomplished by having the next three players in line take the floor while the squad coming off the floor returns to the opposite end of the line.

VARIATIONS

- For further emphasis on passing, you may even want to eliminate dribbling.
- For large classes, you may need to make squads of four or five members.

B rotates on the floor
at this end of the line

B rotates off the floor
at this end of the line

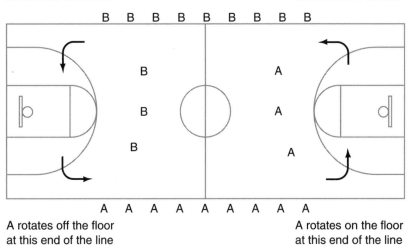

B   B   B   B   B   B   B   B   B

B   A

B   A

B   A

A   A   A   A   A   A   A   A   A

A rotates off the floor
at this end of the line

A rotates on the floor
at this end of the line

CHAPTER 7

TACTICS AND TEAMWORK

Pulling a team together is a challenge that involves not only the skills to play but also interpersonal dynamics. Then the team must face an opponent. This chapter introduces the basics of basketball tactics to students through activities that are intended to teach trust, roles, and personal responsibility. I recommend these activities be used occasionally to reinforce the importance of learning to work together toward a team goal.

Time	National Standards	Grades
5-7 minutes per game	1, 2, 5, 6	3-6

OBJECTIVES

1. Move the ball down the court with short passes rather than long passes or the dribble
2. Move without the ball to open passing lanes
3. Make an entry pass into the free-throw lane

EQUIPMENT

One ball per game, flags for each student

DESCRIPTION

1. Form two teams (four teams if you are using two crosscourts). Each student puts on a flag.
2. Explain to the students that they are going to play a game similar to football. A touchdown is scored by passing the ball down the length of the court and into the lane without dropping it or having it stolen. A player cannot be in the lane for more than 3 seconds.
3. If the ball is dropped or intercepted, or a lane violation occurs, possession goes to the other team who takes it from the spot and begins to move the ball to score.
4. A player has 3 seconds (5 for levels three and four) to pass the ball before the other team is allowed to pull the player's flag, resulting in interception of the ball by the other team. The player replaces his or her flag immediately.
5. A player cannot travel (take more than two steps for levels four through six; three for level three) but can pivot instead.
6. Defenders can be no closer than 3 feet (1 meter).
7. Scoring is similar to football. If a team is successful at passing the ball into the lane, the team scores 6 points for a touchdown. For the point-after attempt, the person with the ball may take an uncontested layup (score 1 point for a dominant-

hand layup and 2 points for a nondominant hand layup). Play
to 21 points or 5 minutes and start a new game.

VARIATIONS

- Add restrictions such as the following:
  - Certain types of passes
  - Ball must be passed to at least five people before going into
    the lane
  - Right-handed passes or left-handed passes only
- Use promotions such as these:
  - Score 6 points for the touchdown when six passes are made
    and then shoot the point after.
  - Give extra points for types of plays such as give-and-go or
    screen and roll.

TEACHING TIPS

- Reinforce with students that the best way to move the ball
  down the court and get ahead of the defense is with short
  passes. Long passes are easily intercepted, inaccurate, and
  sometimes difficult to catch.
- Teach kids to maintain floor balance by moving to open areas
  of the court in order to open passing lanes.

44 Spider's Web

Time	National Standards	Grades
12 minutes	5, 6	5-6

OBJECTIVES

1. Compete as a team while working toward a common goal
2. Learn how to communicate well within the team and develop team unity
3. Explore leader and follower roles within the team

EQUIPMENT

Volleyball standards, 100 feet (30 meters) of 1/4-inch (1/2 centimeters) thick rope

DESCRIPTION

1. Create a spider's web by stringing a rope back and forth between two volleyball standards. Attach the rope to the top of one standard, then bring the rope down and across to the other standard, then down and back across to the first standard, and so on until you reach the bottom. Continue stringing the rope across from bottom to top.

2. Explain to the students that they will be facing a challenge that will test their abilities to think and to solve problems. Encourage creativity.

3. Form teams of 8 to 10 players.

4. Tell the students, "Your challenge is to move your entire team from one side of the spider's web to the other without touching the web. If someone touches the web or the poles that person must return and try again. Once your team uses a hole, you can't use that particular hole again. Talk to each other and communicate as a team to get the job done."

5. Tell the class that when you say, "Go!" they will form their teams on a particular side of the web and begin the activity. You will be the judge to see if they have touched the web or poles.

6. Say, "Go!" and begin the activity.

- The Spider's Web and the next two activities (Logjam Relay and Blind Square) require that students work cooperatively and creatively to solve the problems as they are presented. Therefore, give minimal instructions and get the students started. Circulate to clarify instructions but do not give clues as to how to solve the problem.
- Hold a debriefing session following each of these lessons to discuss the following ideas that these activities address:
  - Leaders and followers
  - Communication levels and types (each activity requires different types of communication: verbal and nonverbal, visual, tactile, and so on)
  - Cooperation and success depends on working together

VARIATION

Combine the Spider's Web activity with the next two all in one lesson if there is time to complete all three, and then hold a debriefing session.

Time	National Standards	Grades
12-15 minutes	5, 6	5-6

OBJECTIVES

1. Compete as a team while working toward a common goal
2. Learn how to communicate well within the team and strengthen team unity
3. Explore leader and follower roles within the team

EQUIPMENT

24 2- × 4- × 12-inch (5- × 10- × 30-centimeter) wooden blocks

DESCRIPTION

1. Make three stacks of eight blocks on one sideline of a basketball court.
2. Explain to the students that they will be facing a challenge that will test their abilities to think and solve problems. Encourage creativity.
3. Form squads of 8 to 10 players.
4. Tell the students, "Your challenge is to move all team members across the river (that is, to the opposite sideline) using a logjam (wooden blocks). Your team will be given two fewer logs than the number of team members. If a player touches the floor, it is like falling in the river and the team must start over. The last person must take the blocks with him or her to the other side. Sliding or throwing the blocks back is not allowed. You will have 2 minutes to talk out your strategy before the game begins. Once the game begins your team can no longer talk."
5. Tell students that you are starting the 2-minute timer, so they should begin to strategize now. When the timer expires tell them, "On my signal you may begin, but remember, no talking once you start. Go!"

TEACHING TIPS

- This activity is nearly impossible to complete without students being willing to support one another physically. It may be necessary to give a hint to teams that are trying to cross as individuals.

- Hold a debriefing session following the activity (see teaching tips in activity 44).

- It is common for a team to abandon the last player, and, almost always, as the final person is trying to gather the blocks he or she falls. Then, just as predictably, the team members start to pick on this player for failing. Point out that the other team members abandoned their teammate and the failure thus belongs to the whole team, not just the last person taking the blocks to the other side. This realization provides a powerful object lesson that the players won't win unless they all work together as a team.

46 Blind Square

Time	National Standards	Grades
12 minutes	5, 6	5-6

OBJECTIVES

1. Compete as a team while working toward a common goal
2. Learn to communicate well within the team and strengthen team unity
3. Explore leader and follower roles within the team

EQUIPMENT

Three lengths of 100 feet (30 meters) of 1/4-inch (1/2 centimeter) thick rope each with its two ends tied together, one blindfold for each student

DESCRIPTION

1. Explain to the students that they will be facing a challenge that will test their abilities to think and solve problems. Encourage creativity.
2. Form groups of 8 to 10 players.
3. Place a piece of rope (with both ends tied together) in the middle of the space being sure that there are no tangles. Place 8 to 10 blindfolds around the perimeter of the rope pile.
4. Tell the students, "This challenge is to be done while blindfolded and without talking. Your team must hold onto the rope and form a square with the rope. When I say, 'Go!' form a circle around the rope pile, pick up a blindfold, and put it on. No talking is allowed from this point on. And, go!"
5. When the time is up, have the students remove their blindfolds and see how they did.
6. If time allows, assign a new shape such as a triangle or a figure 8 and repeat the activity.

Hold a debriefing session following the activity (see teaching tips in activity 44).

47 Freeze

Time	National Standards	Grades
7-10 minutes	1, 2, 5	2-5

OBJECTIVES

1. Begin to explore defensive positioning
2. Understand how to defend without becoming too aggressive

EQUIPMENT

One ball per partnership

DESCRIPTION

1. Explain to the players the concepts of offense and defense. Offense is trying to score, and the closer you are to the basket the easier it is to score. Defense is trying to keep the offensive player from scoring by staying between that person and the basket.

2. Explain that any physical contact will result in a foul. Explain that in order to do this, defenders must move their feet to stay between the offensive player they are guarding and the basket.

3. Divide class into partners. Partners begin one-on-one play at one of the baskets. One or two partnerships may play at a single basket if space is a problem.

4. On your whistle all players freeze.

5. Switch roles after each made basket and after the freeze whistle.

6. Scoring in this game does not come from scoring baskets but instead is as follows: If the offensive player is closer to the basket than the defender, the offensive player gets a point. If the defender is closer to the basket, the defensive player gets a point.

VARIATION

Initially, the emphasis is on being closer to the basket. Later, points can be awarded for assuming the correct defensive position as well as being closer to the basket. Scoring from baskets may be added to the "freeze" points for older players.

Author: Bob Wright; adapted with permission of PE Central (www.pecentral.org), the premier Web site for physical educators.

48 Red Light, Green Light

Time	National Standards	Grades
5-7 minutes	1, 2, 5, 6	5-6

OBJECTIVES

1. Apply two-person skills of screen and roll
2. Read defensive adjustment and react accordingly

EQUIPMENT

Two balls and one cone

DESCRIPTION

1. Players are lined up as indicated in the diagram. You, as coach, serve as the lone defender. The post player is the teammate of the player with the ball. The post player runs a shallow *C* path to set a screen for an imaginary defender (cone) set in front of the ball handler. The ball handler must make a jab step away from the coming screen and then V-cut around the pick to drive to the basket.

2. Decide to (a) stay with the screener or to (b) jump out on the ball handler who is driving to the basket.

3. If you choose to stay with the screener, this is a green-light situation and the ball handler drives to score (see figure *a*). If you jump out to stop the drive, the ball handler executes a two-foot jump stop and throws a push-bounce pass to the roller (the screener becomes the roller once the ball handler drives past the screen; see figure *b*).

4. Have students practice this activity from both wings and the top of the key. Also, students should practice setting screens on both sides of the defender so that the ball handler learns to go both ways. Once students have learned this drill, break them into groups of three and send them to separate baskets to practice each of the positions of screener and roller, rotating every time.

a

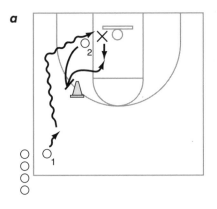

b

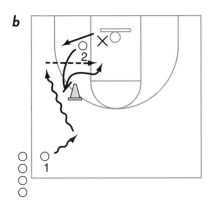

Time	National Standards	Grades
7-10 minutes	1, 2, 5, 6	5-6

OBJECTIVES

1. Begin to build skills that will lead to running an offense
2. Practice and refine skills within a structured offense

EQUIPMENT

Two balls

DESCRIPTION

This layup progression is used to build an offense at the same time as students practice layups from a variety of positions on the court. This is one time when taking turns is necessary. Previous activities focused on maximizing practice repetitions whereas this progression focuses on the performance of specific skills. The following list describes the specific skills and their progression and describes what you, as coach, should be doing in each skill practice. It is important to focus on only one thing at a time and then move on. Instruct the players to try to perform the skill at game speed but only as fast as they can do it correctly.

1. Eyes Up: Coach is located in position C, looking directly at the player's eyes as he or she approaches the basket to execute a layup. The player's eyes should be up, looking at the top corner of the backboard square throughout the entire drive to the basket. Young players tend to watch the ball or look up and down from the ball to the backboard.
2. Fewer Dribbles: Fewer dribbles allow less time for the defense to adjust. Encourage players to take no more than two dribbles inside the three-point line when executing a layup.
3. Give-and-Go Layups: Coach moves out wider on the floor and receives a pass from the player who cuts to the basket (see figure *a* on page 120). The player times his or her footsteps so as to receive the ball in stride and shoot the layup without

a dribble. Have students work on a variety of passes (chest, bounce, overhead). Notice that these first three drills have moved from the slower skill of many dribbles to fewer dribbles, then to no dribbles.

4. Bust-A-Move (V-Cut): Coach is located in position C, the shooting line moves to the middle of the court, and the rebounding line moves to the baseline. Coach receives a pass from the shooter who jogs toward the weak side of the floor where the shooter then plants the outside foot and executes a V-cut, sprinting down the lane. The cutter receives the ball in stride and shoots a layup without a dribble (see figure *b* on page 120).

5. Shoot the "Jimmy": This skill is practiced like the V-cut just described, but have the cutter receive the ball and shoot the jump shot inside the lane.

6. Red Light, Green Light: The coach plays the part of a post defender. His or her "man" executes a shallow C-cut to set a low-side screen for the ball handler on the wing. Use a cone to be the defender. The coach can stay with the offensive player who is setting the screen or can jump out to stop the cutter driving to the basket. The ball handler must make a read as to what the defender is doing. If the defender (coach) stays with his or her "man," this is a green light and the defender drives for the layup. If the defender (the coach) jumps out to stop the player's drive, the defender passes the ball to the roller who is in the mid post (see figure *c* on page 120).

7. Screen Away: The point guard passes to either wing and sets a screen for the weak-side wing. The weak-side wing makes a V-cut away from the screener at the same time the screen is being set. He or she then cuts off the screen toward the high post for the jump shot. The screener rolls to the low post. The wing with the ball makes the read and passes to the open player (cutter or roller depending on who was left unguarded).

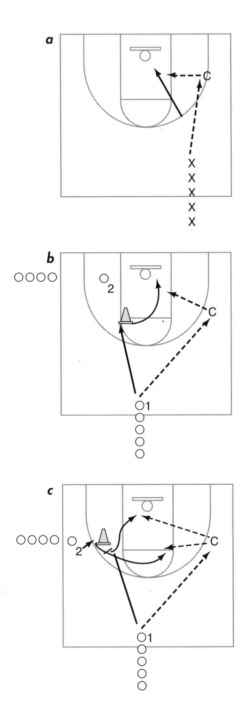

Time	National Standards	Grades
7-12 minutes	1, 2, 5, 6	5-6

OBJECTIVES

1. Apply skills to run or defend the fast break successfully with a numbers advantage
2. Learn to read defenses and make intelligent decisions on the go
3. Practice moving at game speed

EQUIPMENT

One ball per court

DESCRIPTION

This game begins with a three-against-two fast break from one end of the floor to the other and finishes with a two-against-one fast break coming back.

1. Two players take an "I-up" (front and back) defensive position on the far end of the court.
2. Three lines of players line up behind the baseline. The first player in each line forms a team of three. Because there are two defensive players but three offensive players, the offense is said to "have numbers" (an advantage in the number of players).
3. The coach begins the activity by shooting the ball (use various spots on the floor), and the fast break begins when one of the three offensive players rebounds the ball and makes an outlet pass to the ball side of the floor. The receiver then makes a pass to the middle. While working their way down the floor, players must fill the lanes. When they arrive at the far end of the court, the three offensive players try to make a basket.
4. When a basket is made, the player who made the shot now becomes the sole defender in a two-on-one fast break down to the other end of the court (the previous two defenders become the two offensive players in the two on one).

5. The remaining two offensive players stay at the far end of the court and become the next pair of defenders. The drill is repeated with three new offensive players.

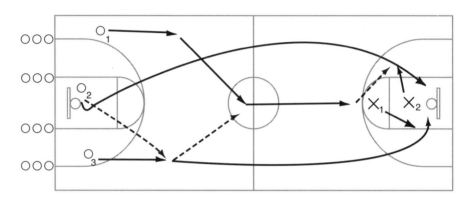

Offensive Rules for Three on Two

- Make a quick outlet pass to the one of the players who did not get the rebound.
- Pass to the middle of the floor, and this player dribbles toward the basket at the far end.
- Fill the lanes (one in the middle and two on the outside).
- Pass the ball to the open teammate for a layup.

Defensive Rules for Three on Two

- Stand in a front and back position or I-up.
- The front person must stop the ball at or near the three-point line.
- The back person must tell the front person to stop the ball and then defend on the first pass.
- The front person, after stopping the ball, retreats to guard the opposite wing. This positioning allows the defender to guard against the layup but gives up the outside shot from the point.

Offensive Rules for Two on One

- Spread apart and force the defender to play the ball handler.
- Use quick passes back and forth so that one player gets a layup.

Defensive Rules for Two on One

- Retreat to half-court, turn, and backpedal to the three-point line.
- Stop the ball near the free-throw line, and then turn and run to the other player and try to intercept the pass. This move is a gamble, but it is surprising to see how often it works.

GLOSSARY

ball side—This term applies to both offense and defense. It is the side of the floor that the ball is on.

baseball pass—A pass that is thrown as one would throw a baseball. It is typically a long pass.

C-cut—A pattern of footwork that is shaped like a "C." It is used to set a lateral or side screen.

chest-bounce pass—Same as a chest pass, except that it is bounced on the floor two-thirds of the distance between the passer and receiver. It is then received at waist height.

chest pass—A pass that covers a short or medium distance. It is thrown with both hands from one's chest to the chest of the intended target.

drop step—A step that a post player often does with his or her back to the basket. It is done by stepping with the foot closest to the baseline toward the basket, allowing the post player to face the basket and shoot a layup. Often, just prior to the drop step, a fake step is used.

elbow—The corner junction of the lane line and the free-throw line.

entry pass—A pass made from the perimeter of the court into the low-post player.

fast break—A breakaway attempt to make a basket by getting down the floor before the defense is in position.

filling the post—A player (usually a center) establishing position at either the low post or high post.

gamelike—A fun, lighthearted activity with an element of competition.

game situation—A more competitive situation that simulates the actual game setting or atmosphere.

give and go—A player passes the ball to a teammate, immediately moves to a new position on the floor, and then receives a pass back.

help side—A defensive term meaning the side of the floor that the ball is not on and from which defensive help will come.

high post—The position on or near the free-throw line.

I-up position—Two defenders should align themselves in a front-to-back position (resembling the letter "I") when facing three or more offensive players.

key—The rectangular area in front of the basket. There are special rules which apply to this area.

low post—The position on one of the two low lane blocks. It is usually occupied by the player who is playing the position of center on the team.

outlet pass—The first pass made once a defensive rebound is secured. It is usually thrown toward the sideline or out from the center. It can also be the first pass to initiate a fast break.

penetration—This occurs when a perimeter player makes a drive into the lane. Once a player has penetrated, he or she may shoot or pass depending on how the defense adjusts. See Red Light, Green Light for a further explanation.

pick—See screen.

post flash—A post player cuts toward the ball either across or up the lane.

rebound—A missed shot that bounces back into play. Either team can regain possession this way.

reverse pivot—A change of direction skill accomplished while dribbling. It involves pivoting on the front foot backwards or away from the defender.

roll(er)—Once a teammate uses the screen, the screener is free to roll toward the ball or the basket. Often, this person is open, which provides a second option for the offense.

screen—A two-person skill designed to eliminate a defender for a split second, enough time to gain an offensive advantage. The screener uses his or her body to block (or screen) the movement of a defender so that a teammate can break free. The screener can set a back screen or a side screen. Once the screen is set, the screener becomes a roller, another offensive threat. The teammate for whom the screen is being set is called the cutter. The cutter must take his defender away from the oncoming screen with a V-cut. The cutter tries to cut off the screen as closely as possible so that the defender cannot fight over the top of the screen. The cutter has both hands up and is ready to receive a pass because the screen is only effective for a brief time and he or she must be ready.

triple-threat position—A stance in which a player with the ball is prepared to pass, shoot, or dribble (three options). Assume an athletic stance, move the ball in a triangle from hip to chin to opposite hip. Use your nonpivot foot to jab step, and look to take advantage of the defense with a pass, shot, or dribble drive.

V-cut—A pattern of footwork that is shaped like a "V." It is used to break away from a defender.

vertical—A straight-line path to the basket. A player who is driving to the basket tries to take a vertical path. A defender must not allow the offense to get vertical but rather try to force the offense to move laterally.

weak side—An offensive term that refers to the side of the floor that the ball is not on.

weak-side flash—An offensive player who cuts toward the ball side from the weak side of the floor.

WANT TO CONTRIBUTE?

If you have an activity that you would like to share with the author, please send it to Keven A. Prusak at 221 E RB, BYU, Provo, UT 84602. Or e-mail your submissions to keven_prusak@byu.edu. Be sure to include your contact information!

Name _____

Address _____

Telephone number _____

E-mail _____

Activity

    Time:

    National standards:

    Grades:

    Objectives:

    Equipment:

    Description:

    Variations or teaching tips:

ABOUT THE AUTHOR

Keven A. Prusak, PhD, is an assistant professor of physical education pedagogy at Brigham Young University in Provo, Utah. He has been working with youth for the past 18 years. Prusak's area of expertise is the study of motivation in physical education. He believes that physical education teachers and youth sport coaches should strive to create a positive and successful experience for all kids. As a professor of physical education, Prusak prepares teachers and coaches to teach in the public school setting.

Prusak received the 1990 Outstanding Teacher Award from the Box Elder School District and the 2002 Lawrence F. Locke Dissertation Award. He regularly makes presentations and conducts workshops for physical educators across the country.